Slouching
towards
Birmingham

Slouching towards Birmingham

Shotgun Golf, Hog Hunting,
Ass-Hauling Alligators,
Rara in Haiti, Zapatistas,
and Anahuac New Year's in Mexico City

Michael Swindle

Frog, Ltd.
Berkeley, California

Published by Frog, Ltd.
Frog, Ltd. books are distributed by
North Atlantic Books
P.O. Box 12327
Berkeley, California 94712

Cover and text design
by Brad Greene
Printed in the United States
Distributed to the book trade
by Publishers Group West

North Atlantic Books' publications are available through most bookstores. For further information, call 800-337-2665 or visit our website at www.northatlanticbooks.com.

Substantial discounts on bulk quantities are available to corporations, professional associations, and other organizations. For details and discount information, contact our special sales department.

Library of Congress Cataloging-in-Publication Data

Swindle, Michael, 1947–
    Slouching towards Birmingham : shotgun golf, hog hunting, ass-hauling alligators, Rara in Haiti, Zapatistas, and Anahuac New Year's in Mexico City / by Michael Swindle.
        p. cm.
    ISBN 1-58394-116-9 (pbk.)
    1. Swindle, Michael, 1947—Travel. 2. Voyages and travels. I. Title.
    G465.S95 2005
    917.04'53—dc22

                                                                    2004031127
                                                                        CIP

        1 2 3 4 5 6 7 8 9 DATA 10 09 08 07 06 05

For my wife
Linda Williams Swindle

"Trapping the Source: Oren-thology in North Central Mississippi," "Slouching towards Birmingham," "Half-Cocked in Cajun Country," "Hog Wild in the Everglades," "Bayed Solid," "Mulletheads," "Barbwire: Postcards from the Edge of NASCAR'S Infield," "Hollerin'," and "Rara in Haiti," in slightly different form, were first published in *The Village Voice*.

"Sportsman's Paradise Lost" appeared in *Speak* Magazine (San Francisco).

"The 'City Lights Bookstore' of Birmingham, Alabama, Prop. Gene Crutcher: A Remembrance" appeared in *Black & White* (Birmingham).

Contents

Foreword

A few months ago, Michael Swindle and I were sitting on the rooftop patio of the Hotel Isabel in the Centro Historico of Mexico City knocking back shots of Cinco Estrellas and chasing it with Indios when it occurred to me that we had been running partners for going on fifteen years, an association that should in all likelihood maintain until one or the other of us is forced to deal with the devil. "All the way, baby," is how Swindle puts it whenever we part, confirming the pact with un gran abrazo y un beso. Seated on spindly wooden chairs on the sunny rooftop in front of the open door of his twelve-dollar-a-day cuarto watching Mamacita y sus hijas hang wash, similar to the circumstances in which Kerouac wrote much of "Mexico City Blues" atop an apartment building on calle Orizaba in the 1950s, I recalled the first time Michael and I met. He had come to interview me at my hotel in New Orleans for *Details* magazine. We hit it off and just kept on going, first in N.O.—where he lived and still does—and then on the road along the Gulf Coast through Mississippi—where he'd been born—to Alabama—where he'd grown up, to Florida, where I'd spent a large portion of my childhood and adolescence. We wound up at the southernmost point of the United States, Key West, where I'd lived during the 1950s with my mother in the old Casa Marina hotel. One early morning there was a violent thunderstorm and Swindle hit the deck, haunted by heavy flashbacks of Viet Cong rockets shelling Red Beach during the Tet offensive in 1968. He was in the Marines then and it was now twenty years later, but certain experiences are always with us and Michael has—despite having dwelt for decades in the Quartier Cinglant in the Land of La Bas—the memory of Funes.

One Saturday night at the Dew Drop Inn on Lasalle Street in New Orleans, Swindle was dancing with a 300-pound woman named Regina to Too Short when our pal, Prince Vincenzu Duda (a fugitive refugee from the Bucovina), said to me, "Michael really has a talent for enjoying himself, doesn't he?" He does, and his talent does not end there. Whether he's whirling with a big leg woman in the wee wee hours, hunting gators in Terrebone Parish, wagering on fighting cocks in Sunset, Louisiana, or facing off with thuggish mobs in Port-au-Prince, Haiti, Swindle has one hand on the wheel and the other where nobody needs to know. What he wants you to know is contained in this book. Read it straight through—all the way, baby.

—Barry Gifford
November 15, 2004

Barry Gifford's novels include *Wild at Heart*, *Night People*, and *The Sinaloa Story*, which is dedicated to Michael Swindle.

Part 1 —
SPORTS of SORTS

TRAPPING the SOURCE: Oren-thology in North Central Mississippi

(In Memory of OREN SWINDLE, Sgt. U.S. Army WW II, 1921–2002)

My Uncle Oren wasn't exactly overjoyed when I called and told him I wanted to go out trapping with him—I am generally considered a city slicker by my rural relatives. The season was almost over, he wasn't catching much, and the weather was wet and cold. "Fact is, son, I've been thinking about throwing it in," he growled over the phone. "It's getting where it ain't worth it. There just ain't enough room in Mississippi anymore for animals *and* people."

If that was the way he really felt, I argued, then that was all the more reason I should get up there and see him in action, and after a little more cajoling on my part and a little more grousing and cussing about the sorry state of things on his part, Oren gave in and said, "Aw hell, come on."

I gunned my fifteen-year-old rust-and-white Volvo station wagon onto the interstate toward Laurel, Mississippi, and turned onto two-lane Highway 15 North. This route adds time to the 350-mile trip, but it also lays out better scenery: sawmills; catfish ponds ("All You Can Catch—$1.25/lb."); tiny general stores plastered with hand-painted signs advertising Jim Dandy feed, Garrett Snuff, Red Man Chewing Tobacco, red worms for sale, quail farms, and shooting ranches; Primitive Baptist wood frame churches with picnic tables set under stands of oak trees beside family graveyard plots; and crossroad flea markets festooned with Confederate flags that no petitions from college students are likely to bring down any time soon.

Highway 15 winds through two-dog towns and wide spots in the road like Bay Springs (its fallen-in "resort motel" now a gray ghost), Newton, Springer (State Basketball Champions, 1957), Noxapater, Louisville (renowned now, as during the Depression, for its moonshine), and Ackerman (famous for my Uncle Guy Swindle's barbecue joint and produce market), on the way to my ancestral stomping grounds in Choctaw County, outside the small town of Eupora (once famous for its blood feuds, and, no, it's not a misspelling of Europa).

The highway also runs through Philadelphia, where the

Choctaw Indians (who refused to relocate to the Plains states
in the 1880s) have their reservation, and where civil rights
workers Goodman, Chaney, and Schwerner were killed
twenty-five years ago. Twenty years ago, I would have
avoided Philadelphia the way I used to avoid the shit-kicking
country radio stations on my car radio dial. The place struck
a nerve in me that later found its most apt expression in
Willie Morris' phrase, the "schizophrenia of race." Even
now, as I cruised along to the music of two of Mississippi's
sons, Jimmie Rodgers and Robert Johnson, I was painfully
aware that Jimmie's music is a bridge back to Uncle Oren's
world, but that he has never heard of Johnson, even though
Johnson and Rodgers and Oren were contemporaries.

In the mid-'60s through the 1970s, I had been estranged
from my roots. From the brutal murders in Mississippi,
where I spent my childhood, to the police dogs and fire
hoses of Birmingham, where I finished elementary and high
school, my feelings of pride in the South were always mixed
with bitterness and disgust. My family never participated
in acts of racial violence, but neither were they marching in
the streets for racial equality. They were the product of their
time and beliefs, and I of mine, and after I reached what the
Bible defines as the age of reason, we didn't converge on
too many issues. Rather than confront the contradictions

they represented to me, I avoided them. In turn, by my absence, I spared them my beard and shoulder-length hair and radical political views inherited, in their minds, from communists or beatniks or Rolling Stones records or God knew where.

I made this trip now because the changes in Mississippi instituted by reformist governors like William F. Winter and Ray Mabus, the death of my father, and my turning forty last year have all affected my perspective: it was time to return to the back-country that I loved as a child and had run from as a young adult.

Uncle Oren, for his part, has always seemed to be playing a game that only he completely understood the rules to. There are fewer and fewer people who farmland trap in the old-style way Oren does, and after more than three decades of being appalled at the thought of catching a living, breathing animal in a steel trap, I suddenly realized I wanted to find out how it was done.

At sixty-seven, Oren has been trapping animals longer than I've been alive, although you couldn't tell it by looking at him: he has the weathered face of a man who's lived most of his life outdoors, but his crack-of-dawn jogging has kept him in the fighting trim he carried into battle during World War II.

Though the gear he uses is the most up to date, Oren learned his trapping techniques as a kid from his uncles in the rolling hills and hollows and the backwoods of north central Mississippi. It is an arcane knowledge that reaches back a hundred years or more—possibly even before the Swindles trekked to Mississippi from Virginia, and maybe even before they left Wales (or Ireland; we never quite got that straight). Oren has added to it from his own experiences over his lifetime.

In truth, Oren and I had never found much to talk about on any subject, and until we climbed into his old Ford pickup to head out for his favorite site, I don't think we'd ever spoken to each other for as much as fifteen uninterrupted minutes (my mother had discouraged me from hanging out too much with Uncle Oren when I was young, because she felt his language was too salty).

But it doesn't take much coaxing to get him talking about trapping.

"For some reason, I was the only one of my generation of the family to take up trappin'," he starts in his high-pitched twang. "The other boys took easily to farmin' and business and seemed to want to forget that their papas had known about things like farmland trappin'. I'd go with my uncles and great-uncles, and I picked up things it'd take a man a lifetime to learn on his own, things hardly anybody I know still uses.

"Of course, things were different when I started out. The men I learned from didn't care all that much 'bout trappin' for money. They were country fellers who had a good time, men who trapped and hunted and fished and farmed just enough to get by. They got by pretty good, I guess, though not by city standards. I don't think any of 'em thought they were missing anything by living in the country."

If you look at his spacious ranch-style brick home with a circular driveway out front and a small well-kept pond off the patio and the Cadillac and pickup truck in the carport, that's a pretty good definition of Oren. You might say he managed to strike a pretty good bargain between civilization and country life, but the key is that he never gave up anything he liked about the country. For twenty-five years, he was one of the biggest cotton farmers in Choctaw and Webster counties. He also grew corn and soybeans, and raised cattle and hogs, until he retired in 1976.

Like so many men who wrestled a living from the earth, Oren was not ready to go gentle into his golden years. Retirement didn't mean a decrease of activity, only a shift of energy from something he *had* to do to something he *wanted* to do. Trapping, which he hadn't had much time for during his farming years, was a natural thing for him to turn to. It is hard, time-consuming work, not much easier than plowing or harvesting. In a way, it *is* plowing and harvesting.

I've never asked him in so many words—I doubt if he'd be able to answer me if I did—but I think what motivates him is the challenge of it, the contest of wills with wild animals. The last thing on their list of priorities is to end up in somebody's trap, and Oren spends his waking hours matching his wits with foxes and pitting his wiles against coyotes. None of the animals Oren traps are endangered species—*he's* the endangered species himself, and likely he'll take most of his trapping secrets with him.

Trapping season in Mississippi runs only from December to mid-February, but Oren spends the rest of the year getting ready for it. He regularly scouts the territory he traps, searching for tracks that tip him off on what animals are around and what trails they're using.

"Animals are jest like people," Oren explains. "They have certain routes they take from one place to another, foragin' for food or lookin' for a mate. They have favorite feedin' grounds—jest like people."

All animals have scent, or musk, glands. (In the beaver, *Castor canadensis*, these glands are called, naturally enough, *castors*, and they are as big as your fist.) Oren cuts these glands out of animals he traps and saves them for scent lures.

"My base ingredient for my lures is a fish oil I make," he confides. "You stuff some small fish—'bout bait size or a little bigger—into a jug and let 'em decompose. Then you mix different musk glands with the fish oil, dependin' on what you're after. I use mink and beaver, but mostly I use muskrat. It seems like *everything* is crazy 'bout muskrat. By God, you can make 'em climb a tree for it!"

The fact is, if you're not a wild furbearing animal, the aroma of these ingredients—rancid fish oil and aged musk glands—is likely to make you so nauseous you'd climb a tree to get some fresh air. For this reason, most trappers use commercially prepared scents, which work just as well. Not Oren. Whether he makes his own out of hardheaded self-reliance, or simply because he's proud that he knows how, is anybody's guess. Maybe it just boils down to aesthetics.

The traps themselves come in a variety of types and sizes, none of which look like the saw-toothed monsters in Saturday morning cartoons. Indeed, steel traps without smooth jaws have been outlawed in virtually every state where trapping is allowed. Oren uses leg-hold traps for everything except beavers. For beavers, which for the last few years have been his main target, he uses what is called a killer-type, or conibear, trap. It's considered one of the more humane traps, because it is a body-gripper, capturing and killing the animal quickly.

"The biggest problem," Oren says, "is domestic animals wanderin' into them. You get around dogs some by using jump sticks—a bent briar or sapling or something like that—to make a dog jump over your trap. You see, dogs when they're out runnin', they will normally go *over* things, where wild animals naturally go *under* things. But cats, well, you know how cats are. You're just gonna catch some goddamn cats."

The conibears Oren uses consist of two 10 x 10-inch square frames, made of $1/4$-inch round steel wire, that are pulled into an open position against a spring and held by a metal latch against a trigger. When an animal makes contact, the spring is released and the frames reverse to trap whatever is inside.

To me, they are nothing but large Chinese puzzles, and though I learned to make booby traps in the Marine Corps, and to fieldstrip and reassemble an M-16 blindfolded, Oren had to take the conibear away from me before I broke my arm trying to set one.

Before setting his traps, Oren boils them in vats made from fifty-gallon oil drums. This serves several functions. New traps are covered with a light layer of oil, which the boiling removes, along with its odor. For old traps, it removes any residue left over from the previous season. Oren throws walnut shells into the boiling water, which dyes the traps brown and camouflages the shiny spots. He adds enough paraffin to create a layer of an inch or two on the surface of the water. After the traps have boiled long enough, Oren pulls them slowly through the melted paraffin, evenly coating each one. This assures quick action and covers the odor of the steel.

Oren keeps his traps in storage baskets until he is ready to use them, and he wears rubber boots and gloves when he sets them. He won't let me within ten feet of where the traps are set, worried that my scent will drive animals away.

"Coyotes are the worst I've ever seen to pick up the scent of steel," Oren tells me. "They won't go anywhere near it. When I'm settin' traps for them now, I've got to where I set the trapline along a barbed-wire fence to throw 'em off. And those rascals can pick up human scent for at least twenty-four hours."

Running the traps (checking them later) turns out to be the anticlimax Oren had warned me it would be so late in the season. Our catch was one smallish beaver, and it gave the lie to the conibear, "killer," trap. The beaver was still alive and Oren had to finish it with his hickory "killing stick," carried for just this purpose. One sharp blow was all it took.

That's also all it took to cure me of my desire to be a trapper. The furbearers of Mississippi have nothing to fear from me. For one thing, at the hour Oren starts trapping, about daybreak, I'm more likely to be going to bed than jumping out of it. For another, I just don't ever want to be in the position of having to crack a beaver's head with a hickory stick. I guess I feel about that the way Roy Blount Jr. does about living where all the road signs have bullet holes in them—I kinda like the general idea of it, but I don't want to feel obliged to put them there.

On the other hand, I can now admit there is a part of me—something so deep down it's beyond surgical removal—that connects to the simple brutalities of the country. I look at Oren, his blue eyes squinting into the sunset as he drives us back to the woodframe skin-house that squats in the pasture behind his home, and come to the realization that some of the things that once bothered me most about my family are the very things I now hold dear. I may not agree with all their practices, but I admire their qualities: they are hard-working people, full of rough humor and pride. They are occasionally wild-assed, sometimes mean, often wise, and always possessed of a pig-headed determination to let the other players know a Swindle is in the game.

Uncle Oren asks me, out of the blue, breaking my reverie, "How long you been livin' in New Orleans now?"

"Six years," I reply.

We bounce over a few bumps in the dirt road before he speaks again.

"You know your way around pretty good? I mean, if somebody set you down in any part of it, would you know how to get back to where you live?"

The question, whether he meant it to or not, raises my spirits. I might be the third leg along Oren's creek banks and deep woods, but he in turn is intrigued by the game I hunt and the urban trails I've mastered in the Crescent City that has lured the likes of Lafcadio Hearn, George Washington Cable, Sherwood Anderson, William Faulkner, and Walker Percy.

"Yes," I say, a smile creeping across my face, "yes, I could do that."

SLOUCHING towards BIRMINGHAM

Of all the great football rivalries—Army-Navy, Texas-Oklahoma, Notre Dame-Southern Cal, Michigan-Ohio State, Oklahoma-Nebraska, Harvard-Yale, Rutgers-Princeton—the greatest of all is Alabama-Auburn. It is also the only one whose loyalties are determined by genetics. Fans on both sides of the ball seem to be born knowing which team they are for.

I, on the other hand, who bleed crimson and white (Alabama's colors), was a late-bloomer. I was ten years old before my Alabama chromosome was triggered. Maybe it was because I got my Y chromosome from a big, hard, fearsome man from Mississippi. Maybe it was because I had spent my early years in the hill country of Mississippi, a time that seems to me even now, over a half-century later, so idyllic as to be almost imaginary.

The fact of the matter is, however, that I was born in Birmingham. My mother's parents lived there, and she refused to give birth to me in Mississippi because she thought of the place as the wild frontier and didn't trust the hospitals. When I told this story to my friend Willie Morris, the late great writer and Mississippian, his eyes widened and he exclaimed, "By God, she was a geographical bigot!"

Anyway, it was 1957 and I was sitting in my father's light green '56 Ford on a Saturday afternoon in late autumn listening to the Alabama-Auburn game on the radio. Like most Southern boys, I loved football, but I hadn't developed a burning zeal for either of the cross-state rivals—I was a Redskins fan. My father had become a dyed-in-the-wool, or perhaps more aptly put, a washed-in-the-blood Alabama fan, and I listened in agony with him on that afternoon as the Auburn War Eagles humiliated the Alabama Crimson Tide, 40-0. As Alabama's situation became more and more desperate, my rooting for them became more and more feverish.

"I wish Alabama could score," I kept saying. "I wish they could somehow win this game."

"Wishing doesn't score points," my father said, never taking his eyes from the road. Then in an even, grim voice he told me that it was worse than I imagined: Alabama had not beat Auburn since 1953. He spoke the scores, 19-6, 28-0, 26-7, like an incantation. He rattled off the names of play-

ers as alien to me at that time as the names of Homer or
Flann O'Brien (the funniest Irish writer ever). He recalled
specific plays from other games where the outcome had
been more just. He spoke of a storied time in the 1930s when
such humiliations were unthinkable, when the name "Crimson Tide" was synonymous with opening a can o' Whup-
Ass on effete California schools, when the great Frank
Thomas coached teams so flawless that Thomas himself
could be forgiven having learned his football from Knute
Rockne at Notre Dame.

Years later, I would look back on that moment and see
my father as a kind of Celtic griot, passing on to me in the
ageless oral tradition important events in the history of our
race. Scenes like this one, I know, are played out in all parts
of the country, but they have special, holy significance in
the South. That Saturday afternoon in 1957 was my introduction into manhood, and my heart and mind and soul
glowed with one thought: that I was, by God, a 'Bama fan.
I still am, so don't expect objectivity here. If you want objectivity, send me to the Oklahoma-Nebraska game.

James Redd, a teenage pal of mine whom I sometimes
helped delivering the afternoon newspaper, brought a new
perspective to the rivalry the day after that 40-0 Auburn
win. "The heavens are out of whack," he said, "when the

unwashed, heathen sacks of shit down at Auburn are kicking our ass the way they are. Something has to be done to restore the rightful order of things."

The elders of the faith in Tuscaloosa were thinking the same damn thing, and they knew where to start work. They got rid of the football coach, J. B. "Ears" Whitworth—the man who benched a senior quarterback named Bart Starr—and went looking for someone stout of heart, quick of mind (and not overly concerned that linebackers be able to translate Tacitus), who could put together some 'Bama teams that would kick the hell out of the War Eagles.

They came home with a fellow named Paul William "Bear" Bryant, whose playing career at Alabama in the mid-'30s had been distinguished primarily by the fact that he played end opposite the great future NFL Hall of Famer, Don Hutson. The Bear lost his first game against Auburn, 14-8, and also lost his last, 23-22. In between, however, he won twenty of twenty-six.

The intensity over the outcome of the Alabama-Auburn game is staggering to visitors from the outside. Traditionally, most of the players on both teams have been from in state and a lot of them either played on the same high school teams together, or against each other. Many of them are from the same hometowns and their parents are friends. And not only are many opposing fans neighbors, many of them are married to each other—that's called a mixed marriage in Alabama. Discussed and cussed all year long, this game carries such emotional freight because it is more than a competition between rival clans; it is the same clan choosing up sides and fighting itself.

An oft-told story is about two brothers, Jimmy and Johnny Davis, of Anniston, Alabama, who did not speak to each other for seven years, after Auburn grad Jimmy accused Alabama alum Johnny of rooting for Georgia in the Auburn-Georgia game. "They finally made up," the *Anniston Star* quoted Jimmy's wife as saying, "but they pretty much avoid each other during the football season."

Controversy has been a hallmark of the rivalry since the first Alabama-Auburn game was played on February 22, 1893. To this day, Alabama counts the game as the last game of the 1892 season, while Auburn counts it as the first game of the 1893 season. The teams did not play each other for forty years in the early twentieth century because of a dispute involving expenses and meal money. The sum in the dispute amounted to 50 cents per player.

That there are people who don't share their feelings for

this match-up is genuinely puzzling to Alabamians. I was shocked, for instance, while stationed in Vietnam in 1967, to discover that the game would not be broadcast on Armed Services Radio. It took me days to find out that Kenny Stabler had slogged through the rain and mud in the final minutes to score the only touchdown of the game and give the Tide a 7-3 victory over Auburn. (That run made me forgive him, more or less, for throwing the ball out of bounds to stop the clock on *fourth* down in the 1965 Alabama-Tennessee game, which resulted in a 7-7 tie.)

Bear Bryant's successor and former Alabama player, Ray Perkins, who has played in both games, said Alabama-Auburn is "bigger than the Super Bowl." He created an uproar one year by saying the game couldn't possibly be as important to Auburn coach Pat Dye, because he played *his* college ball at Georgia. Perkins, however, managed only a 2-2 record against the War Eagles, and some say that, not his pugnacious personality, was the main reason his contract at Alabama was terminated.

Accustomed to winning, especially against Auburn, 'Bama fans weren't too happy about the choice of Bill Curry to replace Perkins in 1987. At least, that's the impression created by the death threats mailed to Joab Thomas, then-president of the university, when Curry's hiring was announced. Curry's overall losing record (38-46-4) wasn't too promising, but the fact that he was 0-7 against Auburn had Alabama alums sputtering so violently they couldn't talk. In Curry's defense, he had to use *real* college students when he was coaching at Georgia Tech.

Another cause for the anger over Curry was the very fact that he was coming from Georgia Tech, a hated rival in Bryant's early years at Alabama. (Bryant had to wear a helmet as protection against flying bottles during one 'Bama-Tech game at Grant Field in Atlanta.) But this was quibbling, and Alabama fans knew it. The basic reason for hostility to Curry was that he never played for, or coached under, The Bear.

Have no doubt about the mythic status Bear Bryant attained in the state of Alabama. Toward the end of his career, rumors circulated that he might be interested in standing for election as governor. The running line was that The Bear was such a shoo-in that he could outpoll the Pope 30 to 1. (That might have been understating the case. It was long rumored that coach Shug Jordan, the most revered coach in the history of Auburn football and a contemporary of Bryant's, suffered in his recruiting because he was Catholic.)

Trying to coach at Alabama without having a Bryant connection was like having someone named Rabinowitz

trying to head the Mafia. It's not that it *can't* be done, it's
just that a lot of people are going to be dead set against it
from the outset.

To this day, the match-up is called the Iron Bowl, because of
the coal and iron and steel industry that the city of Birmingham was built upon. Call me a mossback, but I just can't
go along with this. The "Iron Bowl," the real one, was
played at Legion Field in Birmingham for forty years on
the Saturday after Thanksgiving. In 1988, it became a home-
and-home affair, with Auburn planning to play its home
games in a new, expanded stadium on campus. Alabama
favored keeping the game in Birmingham, which it considers a neutral site. Auburn, on the other hand, sees Legion
Field as an Alabama stadium, because the Alabama campus in Tuscaloosa is a mere sixty miles down the road.

It's hard to see why they would think that, unless perhaps it's the twelve-foot bronze statue of Bear Bryant at the
entrance. Hell, 'Bama people say, if Auburn had a coach
who won 323 games, they'd put up a statue of him too. So
Alabama fans viewed Auburn's feelings in this matter as
springing from a "cow college" inferiority complex and a
shithead reason to kill a tradition.

The city of Birmingham offered the teams an extra
$125,000 not to move the game, but Auburn was expecting
an additional $250,000 in increased revenue from the move
to its own stadium. Prizzi's family would feel at home at
Auburn: honor is fine, but the bottom line is money.

I made a pilgrimage to see the last authentic Iron Bowl in
1987, and I remember it well.

The irony of that year's match-up was that Auburn coach
Pat Dye was once an assistant coach for Bryant at Alabama.
An indication of how convoluted the relations in this rivalry
are is that when Ray Perkins left Tuscaloosa to take his first
coaching job in the NFL, he sold his pickup truck to Dye.

Game day in Birmingham was gray and somber. An hour
into the game, the lights had to be turned on at Legion
Field. The day matched the mood of the many fans who
were mournful about the end of a forty-year tradition. The
somberness of the occasion seemed to affect the players on
both teams. After the excitement of so many games in recent
memory, tight battles won or lost in the final seconds of the
game (the previous five games had been decided by a total

of twelve points), a dull one was bound to crop up, and that proved to be the case. The game produced no legends that would be passed on to schoolboys over pecan pie at Thanksgiving dinner—like Joe Namath being benched for the game in his senior year, or Ken Stabler breaking four tackles in a downpour to score the only touchdown in the year I was at Red Beach, outside Danang.

This would not be a replay of Auburn's come-from-behind victory in 1972, on two blocked punts run in for TDs, or The Bear's last regular season game in 1983, played as a tornado headed straight for Legion Field. (Keith Jackson and Frank Broyles were calling the game for ABC and began to joke about how no one in the crowd was leaving as the twister bore down on Birmingham. The joke died in their throats as they realized tornadoes don't make exceptions for network announcers.) This would not be the 1984 game when Auburn's Bo Jackson ran the wrong way on fourth and goal, and Alabama won 17-15. And it certainly would not even be close to the 1985 game, without question the greatest college football game ever played, which saw junior place kicker Van Tiffin boot a fifty-two-yard field goal with no time left on the clock to put Alabama up 25-23.

An old-fashioned defensive battle, the tension in this game was over whether anyone would score or not.

Auburn did—one TD in the second quarter and one field goal in the second half. Auburn 10, Alabama 0.

But when I said a dull game was inevitable, I meant, of course, dull for an Alabama-Auburn game. For mythic match-ups like Oklahoma-Texas and Michigan-Ohio State, this would have been positively a thriller. Exactly ten inches spread over three plays made the difference. In the first quarter, Alabama had a fourth and one at the Auburn 46; fullback Bo Wright was stopped exactly two inches short of a first down. In the second quarter, Alabama missed a fifty-three-yard field goal when the tip of the ball grazed the left upright, ricocheted off the crossbar, and landed in front of the goal posts—let's call that a two-inch miss. Later in the second quarter, Alabama linebacker Derrick Thomas blocked a punt at the Auburn nine. Three plays later Bobby Humphrey, probably the best running back in the nation at that time, was slammed to the artificial turf six inches short of the Auburn goal line; Bill Curry chose to go for the TD on fourth down, but a pass from freshman Jeff Dunne fluttered harmlessly out of the end zone. That's it: ten inches, one game, one point per inch.

After the game, I went to Cosmo's Pizza, on Birmingham's

Southside. As I stared sorrowfully out the plate glass window at the quiet street below, one of the co-owners, Stanley Schafferman, came over to my table. "If Alabama had won the game," he said, "it would look like Mardi Gras out there. Auburn fans just seem to head for home."

There is a dialectic there about Alabama versus Auburn fans, but after a 'Bama loss, I was too depressed to go into it. I could only squint into the darkness and hope that somewhere out there was another Bear, slouching towards Birmingham, a new era waiting to be born.

SPORTSMAN'S PARADISE LOST

Going hunting and fishing with my father was *not* a Faulknerian ceremony of passage. Looking back on the brief time I spent at these activities in the wilds of hill-country Mississippi, one day was like a week at Parris Island. A quail hunt was a forced march, beginning before sunrise and ending past sunset, the more briars to wade through the better. Sitting in a fishing boat on Lake Grenada, waiting and waiting and waiting for the bite that never came, was like being on an amphibious ambush, requiring an enforced silence and a sense of optimism that were simply alien to my basic nature. The man was serious, I'm telling you, *serious* about his hunting and fishing. And I just broke under the strain. I couldn't take it, so I turned to other things.

Still, experiences like that stick with a man. And if he's a man in his "middle years," he can start making a case to himself that his turning away from these rituals of Southern manhood has made him a lesser person. This can be risky business, if you live, as I do, in Louisiana, where the state slogan, proudly stamped into our car tags, is "Sportsman's Paradise." Because in Louisiana, if you put your mind to it, you can go alligator hunting.

Now, I'll be the first to admit that my credentials for such an enterprise are pretty slim. My previous encounters with alligators have been limited to a visit to a tourist "gator farm" in St. Augustine on a family vacation when I was ten years old (you could get your picture taken in a small wagon hitched up to one of the reptiles, and yes, I did); IZOD shirts; and a taxidermied alligator head I convinced my hesitant mother to buy me for my birthday one year to go with the Brazilian piranha, Honduran turtle, domino-playing Mexican frogs, and a pair of Oklahoma fighting cocks I've acquired over the years. (I ask friends not to give me ties for Christmas.)

Despite this obvious handicap, I convinced myself that going on an alligator hunt would be a *redemptive* experience. That by going, I would not only escape my urban treadmill of word processors, fax machines, and call waiting, but that I would reconnect on a spiritual level with the lost communion with my father in those long ago years in the backwoods of Mississippi.

Besides, fifty square miles of Louisiana's coastline is

annually eroding into the Gulf of Mexico, approximately one acre every ten minutes. With the Gulf only fifty miles from New Orleans, I felt it would be a good idea to get familiar with dealing with alligators, so I'd know what to do when the bastards come creeping onto my patio to snack on my well-fed orange cat.

The first thing I discovered, however, was that alligator hunting was not something you simply decide to do and then go do it. Since they were removed from the endangered species list in Louisiana in 1972, the season for alligators has been restricted to a thirty-day period in early fall, and you have to have a state tag from the Department of Wildlife and Fisheries to bag one. DWF issues tags based on population studies of the gators. About 25,000 are issued each year, but only to landowners or leaseholders based on acreage. A coastal marsh area of five to ten acres will support one gator, and the little 165 x 16-foot lot my Victorian shotgun house sits on in New Orleans doesn't command the first tag.

Through an artist friend of mine who had recently completed a commission that entailed casting a ten-foot bronze gator from the (stuffed) real thing, I was able to secure an invitation to go out on the opening day of gator season with a seventy-five-year-old Cajun trapper, gator hunter, and visionary accordion player.

I followed the "country directions" out of New Orleans on State Highway 90 toward the Gulf Coast marshland and bayous of Terrebonne Parish, about sixty miles south of the city as the pelican flies: Take the first Raceland/Houma exit and head south. Take a left at the first water tower ("Blue Bayou," it turns out). A left at the next water tower ("South Terrebonne," ditto). Go straight until you see the sign directing you to Pointe au Chien and go on out that two-lane road until you see Dovie Naquin's mailbox on your right.

I took the turn-off onto the two-lane blacktop that would lead me to Pointe au Chien, which means Dog Point in English. It is a peculiarly ironic name, because a truism of the bayou is that where there are alligators, you *never* see stray dogs.

To my right was the flat, disappearing marshland, dotted here and there by straggly stands of dead cypress trees, killed by salt water intrusion, silhouetted against the hazy, early morning southern skyline. Just off the roadway on my left wound Bayou Pointe au Chien on its way to Timbalier Bay and the Gulf, and across it the watery swampland of Lafourche Parish stretching northward as far as the eye could see.

Mr. Longfellow rambled on in "Evangeline" about "the forest primeval," but his mind's eye must have been up in

Mississippi. It was *not*, I assure you, on the nothing-but-horizon south Louisiana landscape I was driving through.

It was going on eight o'clock in the morning, as Dovie and I made our way from his raised cypress house to his small, open boat shed. We settled down in his pirogue, or "mud-boat," a twelve-foot flat-bottomed craft tapered at both ends, a foot and a half deep, and three feet at its widest point. He pointed proudly to his new eight-horse-power motor, saying it was the smallest you could buy that had an electric starter. Checking his lines requires a number of stops, and he felt he'd pull-started enough engines for one lifetime.

This was a late start for Dovie, a small, wiry fellow looking far younger than his seventy-five years, with an animated face that could not mask his disappointment at the discovery that my French was too limited to carry on a decent conversation. He kicked in all eight horses and headed us out over the open water toward the marshland that fifteen years ago was a continuation of his backyard, but now takes a good half hour to reach by boat.

Dovie throttled down as we entered the claustrophobic world of the marsh proper. Marsh grass towered above our heads and had to be continually brushed back from

our faces and bodies, as we wound slowly along the narrow watery pathways the Cajuns call *trainasses*. The smell
permeating the marsh, where the water in most places is
only a foot or two deep, was something unto itself. Not
disagreeable, exactly, but cloying and unavoidably funky.
The kind of smell that could make a self-respecting
amphibian want to alter gills and fins into lungs and arms
and legs, climb out of the ooze, and head for the nearest
shopping mall.

His limit was twenty-seven alligators, and Dovie had
set out thirty-one lines the day before the opening day of
the season, which you are allowed to do. These lines consisted of a fifty-foot length of quarter-inch rope attached
to a strong steel hook. Each line was tied securely to a stake,
a short length of 2 x 4 cut to a point on one end that was
driven into the ground and served as an anchor. The lines'
slack was coiled loosely next to the stake, out of gator-sight
in the brush or grass at each site. Then baited hooks were
draped through a forked tree branch jabbed into the bank
so that they hung temptingly above the surface of the water.
Dovie used chunks of nutria meat as bait.

Nutria, the hamburger helper of the swamp, are brown
furbearing beaver-like rodents about the size of a small
housedog, with long orange upper front teeth. (I swear!)

They were introduced into this country in 1937 by E. A. Mc-Ilhenny, an avid naturalist and founder of the company that makes Tabasco-brand pepper sauce. On a trip to Argentina, he was given thirteen nutria, which he brought home to Avery Island.

In a very short time, E. A. had forty-seven nutria. A bigger pen had to be built. And still the nutria keep coming. And of course, a hurricane hit the coast of Louisiana, and all the nutria escaped into the surrounding swamps.

This was not a good thing. The rodents proved so prolific that today they pose a new and dangerous threat to the fragile ecosystem of Louisiana's coastal wetlands. Herbivores with voracious appetites, nutria consume a third of their body weight in vegetation daily, and their favorite meal is marsh grass. Not content to dine on just the shoots, they also pull up the plants to savor the roots. Their numbers are presently so high that the marsh areas where they feed are eroding with alarming quickness into permanent open water, putting them in the ranks of man-made oil and natural gas exploration canals, salt water intrusion, and flood control projects, as the chief causes of wetlands loss.

Nutria have even migrated to canals in Jefferson Parish, west of New Orleans, where their numbers and their eating habits threaten to cave in the canal banks, thereby sabotag-

ing flood control. They are such a nuisance that parish sher-
iff Harry Lee joins his SWAT team on periodic night patrols,
offing the treacherous critters with .22 rifles.

The first three lines Dovie checked were undisturbed, the
bait still dangling over the water. As we approached the
fourth, we could see that the holding branch was down.
Dovie shut off the motor and we coasted up to where the
line trailed off into the water.

"The line don't look too tight," he said. "Maybe some
bird knocked it down."

He grabbed hold of the line and gave it a tug. "Oh yeah,"
he cried out, "we got one!"

But as he tugged on the rope and pulled the gator's head
out of the water, his enthusiasm ebbed a bit, because it was
a small one. Brokers pay for alligator hides by the foot, so
the shorter the gator, the smaller the payday for catching
them. And this one appeared to be only a six-footer.

You can tell the length of an alligator by the size of its
head. The length in inches from its nostrils to its eyes corresponds almost exactly to the entire length of its body in
feet. It's weird, but it's true. You can look it up.

Holding the line in his left hand, Dovie placed the barrel of his .22 rifle over the soft spot at the back of the gator's head and killed it with one shot to the brain. It thrashed for a hot minute, then went belly up and slowly began to sink below the surface.

Dovie sat back down and pulled the gator up until its head rested over the side of the pirogue. He immediately gripped both jaws at the end of the nose with his left hand and tied them shut with a length of cord. All the awesome power of an alligator's jaws is in their closing, so they can lock on to their prey and hold them underwater until they drown. You couldn't pry their jaws open with a crowbar, but once they're closed they can be easily held closed.

"Sometimes they just play dead," Dovie said with a big grin, as he looped the cord around the gator's neck behind the jaws and secured it to the stern of the pirogue to haul it home.

His comment reminded me of a "dead gator" article I had seen in the local paper. Two guys ran over a nine-footer in their car on Highway 90, and after inspecting it, declared it dead. They loaded it into their hatchback and headed home, smacking their lips at the thought of cooking it up with some sauce piquant. A few miles down the road, the "dead" gator regained consciousness and began to thrash around like crazy, trying to get out of the car. The men quickly turned into a handy supermarket parking lot and abandoned the vehicle.

Dovie guided the puttering pirogue down another narrow, twisting *trainasse*, and cut the engine as we entered an open area. One of his lines was stretched as tight as a piano wire across the lagoon, a sure sign of a hooked gator. Grabbing the line, he slowly pulled the pirogue, hand over hand, toward the spot where the line disappeared onto the far bank. From ten feet away, we could see that the gator had crawled headfirst as far as it could into the brush.

"Look at the tail on him," Dovie said excitedly. "He's a big one for sure."

The problem, as I saw it, was how to get him turned around and back into the water, where he would be easier to manage. This was no problem at all, however, as Dovie saw it.

"Oh no," he told me. "If he's swallowed that hook good, down into his belly, I can bring him to me with two fingers. He's gonna *want* to come to me, 'cause it *hurts*, man."

The hook, as it turned out, was not set in the gator's belly, but firmly in his jaw. It took considerable poking with Dovie's push pole—a long wooden pole forked at one end to gain a hold on the muddy bottom of the marsh—and some hefty tugging to maneuver him into the water. Before he slid from the bank, he emitted a loud, eerie hissing sound that was chilling. The creature was easily over ten feet long, and the pirogue rocked wildly in the wake of his frenzied thrashing. Water was flying everywhere as the bull gator slung his massive, snapping jaws from side to side, in an attempt to dislodge the hook.

As Dovie worked him to the port side of the mudboat, the gator submerged. With the .22 rifle in his right hand, the wiry seventy-five-year-old gave a one-handed pull with all the strength in his 140-pound body. The gator's head broke the surface of the water, and Dovie fired a round. It hit too far forward on the head and ricocheted off the rock-hard plating. He stuck the barrel an inch or so behind the head of the gator and fired again. The gator went quiet in the water. After a third shot to "make sure" the gator was dead, the scene was so calm that all I could hear was my heart pounding.

Dovie bagged three alligators on that opening day of the season: the six-footer, one that was almost eight feet, and the big bull, which measured out at 12 feet. I got bumped on day two, due to the arrival of a friend of Dovie's from Belgium. He *did* speak French.

I wasn't too disappointed though, because when you get right down to it, alligator hunting isn't hunting at all. It's fishing.

Don't get me wrong. I was deeply touched by the hospitality of Dovie and his extended family, in allowing me to share a slice of their lives. The homemade beignets, the smothered potatoes and green beans, and the fresh alligator courtbouillon were beyond compare. And hooking a 12-foot alligator sure beat the hell out of fishing for crappie, perch, or bass, but it still made me think of running trotlines on Lake Grenada.

Rather than being a spiritual reconnection, going out with Dovie only served to make me face up to the fact that there are certain rituals I will forever be outside of.

I would be less than truthful, however, if I didn't tell you that in early fall, or what passes for it in south Louisiana, when the brown shrimp season has ended and the local media begin to focus on the upcoming alligator season with an intensity that rivals that of the football season, there are times when a strong memory comes back to me, just before I drift off to sleep.

It is of an evening down on the fragile, marshy southern edge of Louisiana. Dovie and I are sitting on the front porch of his raised house. He is in his rocking chair, a harmonica rack around his shoulders, playing his button accordion. He is singing a tune he wrote himself, in the plaintive, high-wailing French Cajun style that has a lot in common with Appalachian hill music.

The song tells of the hardships of wrestling a living from the swamps, and the joy of having a good woman to come home to after a grueling day, but its real message is found in the refrain: *"Je me dormi comme un vieux mulet/Quand je va rêver de la cocodrie tout la nuit."*

"I am sleepy like an old mule," Dovie sings. "When I go to bed, I'll dream of alligators all night long."

HALF~COCKED in CAJUN COUNTRY

Never become close friends with a fighter, Hemingway cautioned, because one day you'll have to watch him get busted up. Good advice, but Hemingway didn't know how lucky he was. At least he never had to cook his friend and eat him.

My paternal grandmother, who lived on a forty-acre farm in Choctaw County, Mississippi, once had a red-and-black farmyard rooster for which she had developed a deep affection. He would follow her around like a puppy, clucking at her and keeping her company as she went about her chores. For everyone else, however, he was a terror, rushing out from some hiding place or other and spurring the hell out of anyone who was happening by. The consensus of the family was that she should get rid of him, but she couldn't quite bring herself to do that.

My number came up one summer morning while chasing yellow butterflies around the yard. I was wearing shorts and he caught me from behind, opening a deep, two-inch gash just above the bend of my right leg. As I shrieked and howled, my parents ran out of the house; my father, in his anger, chased down the rooster and wrung its neck.

I'm sure that in her own way my grandmother grieved for that rooster, but she cleaned him and dressed him, and he rested all fried up on a platter on the supper table that night. As much as my leg still throbbed, I couldn't bring myself to eat a bite of him. Grandmother, if my memory serves, had a breast with gravy all over it.

I was eight years old when that episode took place, but I was reminded of it last year by local news coverage of efforts to make cockfighting illegal in Louisiana. I had been aware, of course, that cockfighting existed, but in much the same way I knew that capital gains taxes exist. Neither bit of knowledge had ever had any real impact on my life.

The next day, I ran across a copy of Charles Willeford's novel, *Cockfighter*, at the French Market in New Orleans. In the middle of the book, Willeford quotes from a letter to the French general Lafayette from George Washington. "It will be worth coming back to the United States," wrote the father of our country, "if only to be present at an election and a cocking main at which is displayed a spirit of anarchy and confusion, which no countryman of yours can understand."

That did it. Elections had brought me no joy over the last decade and I knew the damage a rooster could do to me, so I decided to find out what a couple of them could do to each other.

Although cockfighting is still legal in my state, you won't find any results or schedules listed in *The Sporting News* or *USA Today*. In fact, my initial investigation into this phenomenon convinced me that, as with Gnosticism, most of the information you could gather about cockfighting came from its enemies. A city ordinance forbids the sport in New Orleans, and it is impossible to find magazines like *Grit and Steel*, *Gamecock*, or *The Feathered Warrior*, which are devoted to this particular demimonde. (Ironically, a friend sent me copies from buttoned-down Birmingham, Alabama, where they are easily obtained.) Even these mags, when you get right down to it, are fairly cryptic themselves about the exact location of the cockpits they cover.

And that was my big problem—I didn't have the slightest notion where to find a cockpit. Since I felt time was of the essence, I did what anyone in their right mind would do when stumped about a sports question in New Orleans: I went to the ancient New Orleans Athletic Club and laid

out the situation to my barber, Mike Reese. With barely a
pause for breath, he gave me directions to Cormier's Bar &
Cockpit in the rustic Cajun hamlet of Cankton, Louisiana,
"just up the road from the funky and defunct Jay's Lounge
& Cockpit, the last of the old-time honky-tonks, where bands
like Clifton Chenier and his Red Hot Louisiana Band used
to play long before Paul Simon realized that zydeco was
Authentic American Folk Music." Mike, who used to blow
sax in an R&B band, finished my $11 haircut with a splash
of Pinaud Clubman lotion on the back of my neck and the
warning: "Don't take too much money with you, though,
'cause that shit'll hook you worse than football."

I had gathered from anti-cockfighting editorials that habitués
of the cockpit were invariably depraved, unshaven, hip-
pocket whiskey-toting, dim-witted hillbillies, who exhib-
ited the telltale bulging pop-eyes and four teeth in their
mouths pointing in different directions that indicate too
many cousins bedding down with each other for too long.
(I don't know about you, friends, but this is the kind of stuff
that gets my inquiring mind up around the boiling point.)

The most striking thing about the crowd at Cormier's,
as a result, was how "normal" they looked. For the Cajuns

of the area, cockfights are a community event, often held to benefit the local fire department or some other civic organization. Entire families, some representing three generations, were present: Grampa and Dad sipping Buds, while Gramma and Mom rode herd on the kids with their Pepsis and Elmer's CheeWeez. There were people who through the week worked as bankers, lawyers, doctors, ranch hands, service station attendants, housewives, and dirt farmers. High school couples, the guys in Reeboks and polo shirts and the girls in identical teased-up bouffants, were out for a big Saturday night.

Not that everyone looked like they had just stepped out of the pages of *GQ* or *Vogue*, mind you. I will admit some of them did look a little funny, but you can't fight the fact that cousins *do* get together now and again, and not only in French movies and Walker Percy novels.

Backing your bird with money, whether you are owner, handler, or spectator, is as old as the sport itself, which is old indeed. (Regulations for cockfights have been traced back 3,000 years to ancient India.) Betting is such an integral part of cockfighting that rules prohibiting gambling posted at Cormier's refer to impromptu card or dice games.

Getting a handle on how to bet on fighting cocks is not unlike being thrown into an alligator pond to learn how to swim. The scene is only slightly less intense than trading on the floor of the stock exchange, and is a far cry from the horse track, with its easy-to-read odds board and generally orderly lines at the pari-mutuel windows. Betting at a cockfight is ... well, the word cockers like to use is "democratic," but Washington had it pegged when he mentioned anarchy.

Wagers are made between individuals, on the honor system. Integrity is highly prized in the world of cockers, in part because they are sensitive to the social stigma attached to their passion, and it is extremely rare for someone to welsh on a bet. Offers are aggressively shouted over and over, and accepted with a nod of the head after eye contact is made.

Betting doesn't commence, it breaks out: CALL 25-20 ... CALL 25-20 ... 50 OVER HERE ... 10 OR 20 ON THE RED ... I GOT 50 OVER HERE ... LAY 50-40 ... LAY 50-40 ... CALL 100 TO 80 ... 10 OR 20 ON THE RED ... LAY 10-7 ON THE GRAY... HUNDRED ON THE HATCH... CALL 50 ON THE GRAY...

"Call 25-20" means a person wants to bet the smaller amount against the larger, and "Lay 25-20" means a person will bet $25 to win $20. The person giving the odds (risking the larger amount of money) always gets to choose the cock he thinks will win. To bet any amount "over here" or "over there" simply relates to where the bettor is sitting and on which side of the pit a particular cock may be. "Red," "gray," and "hatch" refer to strains of gamecocks. (Ready to win some money?)

The seventy-ish white-haired gentleman sitting next to me, dressed in a pale blue version of the one-piece polyester jumpsuit that seems to have replaced bib overalls as all-purpose casual wear in the rural South, was a retired elementary school principal. He was there with a chubby friend, Amos, who brought cocks to fight; Amos' chubby wife; Larry, who would handle the cocks in the pit; and Larry's ten-year-old son. We struck up a conversation like old friends. That's the way these folks are. No introductions were made; the two names I know, I picked up in passing. They were a high-spirited, garrulous group, and took me under their wing (so to speak) when I told them this was my first cockfight.

I asked Larry if pushing these birds into fighting wasn't unnecessarily cruel. "That's where people get confused," Larry said, shaking his head. "We don't teach these birds *how* to fight. That's an inborn thing. They'll fight to the death in the wild. All we do with our training is to make sure they're in the best possible physical condition." I was skeptical, but determined to see the evening out.

The first match-up was between a gray cock and a red one. When the principal made a $5 wager on the red cock, "for the sport of it," I asked him how he'd come to that decision.

"I never have liked a gray rooster," he said.

Ah, the scientific method, I thought. The same reasoning I use when playing the ponies.

The gray, in fact, wasn't gray at all, but resembled its opponent except for its blond hackles, or neck feathers, while the "red" cock had more iridescent bronze feathers than red ones. But superstitions about the color of a bird, I later found out, are confined to spectators. The elusive quality of "gameness"—the instinctual urge to battle and domination that drives a cock to fight on regardless of blindness, a broken wing or leg, punctured lungs, or what have you—is what every serious breeder of cocks is after. The color of the bird is of absolutely no consequence to them, which makes things extremely confusing for the non-adept, because any given strain can contain several combinations of colors.

"You get right down to it," Larry chimed in, "a fifty-fifty chance is the best you got in a cockfight. You can take either side you like and still be in a pretty big crowd."

For every theory about gamecocks, there is at least one opposing view. Ask a Cajun, for example, if the cocks that are killed in the pit are ever eaten and they will tell you, "Sure! Finest eating you've ever had." Ask someone else, and you're told they're too tough to eat and only a fool would try to cook one. (I'm inclined to go with the Cajuns; if they can make possums, armadillos, and swamp rats delectable, fighting cocks should be a snap.) As for the "gameness" of a given strain, arguments have been going on for at least 3,000 years, and there is no end in sight.

In the red cock's corner was the place to be that night, however. At the referee's command to "pit," the men released their birds into the center of a large, round, dirt-floor arena that was enclosed floor to ceiling with chicken wire. The red and the gray met in midair three or four feet off the ground in a blast of beating wings and the flashing of the three-inch hand-forged steel gaffs attached to the legs of each cock. The red scored with a brain shot in the air, and the gray hit the ground motionless. If he wasn't dead at that moment, he was within a few seconds, as the red delivered a blur of steel to the fallen cock's head. It had taken the red less time to take out the gray than it took Mike Tyson to finish off Michael Spinks (ninety-one seconds). The big difference was that, unlike the gray, Spinks was

able to walk around and answer questions at a press conference afterwards.

Larry won his first fight easily (well, his cock did the
fighting, but the bond between a cocker and his bird can
get downright metaphysical) and lost his second the same
way. His third time out, the opposing cock hung a gaff in
the chest of Larry's and the birds had to be held down
("handled") to get it dislodged.

"That was a lung shot," the principal told me during the
twenty-second rest period between pittings. "He's already
dead."

I watched as Larry took the cock's head in his mouth
and jerked his own head back in a sucking motion. He did
this a couple of times.

At "get ready," Larry placed his cock on its mark for the
next pitting. The bird's head was wobbling, its beak open
trying to draw air into its lungs. He looked like a goner,
but when his opponent barely missed with a head shot, he
took a staggering side step and landed a killing blow that
put the crowd on its feet, yelling and slamming one another
on the back.

When Larry returned to the stands, I asked him what
he'd been doing with the cock's head in his mouth.

"After he took that gaff to the lungs, I could hear the

death rattle deep in his craw," Larry said between long pulls on a cold beer, "so I just sucked as hard as I could until I felt the clot come loose. I was gonna spit it out, but I was excited and forgot and swallered it."

He looked about as bad remembering his oversight as I felt hearing about it.

By the luck of the draw, Larry's last fight was the final one of the night. He was pitting a sinewy white cock against the fiercest looking cock I had seen all evening, but if he won, he also got the $1,000 purse money for most victories.

When they were pitted, the red and the white bowed their heads to the ground before colliding in midair so hard they both fell back earthward. Regaining their balance, they made a quarter turn on each other and met in another aerial explosion. They hit the ground this time hung up. When they had been handled and the white tried to stand free, it fell over, its right leg obviously broken.

Larry fussed over the bird, but there was nothing to be done, and at the call of "get ready," he set the white on its "mark." When Larry released it at the command "pit," the white's right leg collapsed and he awaited his opponent lying prone in the pit.

Suddenly, I found myself more concerned for the safety of the white than I was for the fifty bucks I had impetuously

bet on him. I cringed when the red cock took one step forward and leaped toward the white's head, its steel gaffs
flashing in the lights. Somehow, the white wriggled out of
the way, and as the red wheeled to attack again, struck first
with a sharp beak to the red's head. The red began to run.

This was the unthinkable—to show lack of "gameness"—
in the world of cocking. It was an affront, not to the owner
or trainer, but to the proud bloodline of the fighting cock
that can be, and is quite often by aficionados, traced until
it disappears down the backloads of antiquity. Consequently,
cocks that run are summarily killed.

As in baseball, however, they get their three strikes. Pitted against the white twice more, the red ran both times,
while the white bobbed on its breast, vainly attempting to
land a blow. That one crack on the red's head had driven
out centuries of instinctual combativeness and left in its
place shame, degradation, and a severely shortened life-
span. The red was taken from the pit to the sound of the
full-throated, triumphant crowing of the white rooster.

"Magic birds," cackled the principal as he stomped out
of the room in a victory dance. "By God, we got magic
birds! One came back from the dead, and another won with
a broken leg!"

I was drawn to cockfighting in part because it *was* a blood sport, but I knew I wasn't the type of fan Willeford wrote about: the man who comes to love the sport so much he has to possess a gamecock of his own, who through pride of ownership has to pit his cock with another one, at which point—win or lose—he's as hooked as a poor crackhead talking to his pipe and calling it by name.

Still, I was glad I'd been able to see it for myself before what cultural anthropologist Clifford Geertz, in his essay "Deep Play: Notes on the Balinese Cockfight," called "the pretensions of puritanism" did away with it—along with boxing, smoking, and abortion. In France, cockfighting is permitted in regions that can demonstrate that the practice is a longstanding cultural tradition. This certainly seems the case in Cajun country in Louisiana, but cockfighting will undoubtedly be outlawed here and throughout America before too long. Its brutality is undeniable and all too visible to those animal rights activists who denounce blood sports over white wine and veal picante.

To tell the truth, I thought I should have felt more remorse than I did about the cocks that were killed. I don't know if it was the memory of my run-in with my grandmother's rogue rooster, or the fact that he wasn't the only chicken I ever saw get its neck wrung or its head chopped off. I do know that in the course of the night I spent at Cormier's, I came to see that fighting cocks don't come to the pit with the excess baggage of court battles with managers and promoters, or, by all reports, any kind of spousal problems. I also saw how fighting cocks face death—with their heads up, their chests out, and a blaze in their eyes. I've never heard of any of their lesser brothers and sisters in the chicken world strutting—fearlessly and defiantly—into the Tyson processing plant.

HOG WILD in the EVERGLADES

There was a thick fog over the land as we crept along in second gear on a two-lane blacktop outside Immokalee, Florida, with an eye out for Jose and Mexican George and the dogs. Like most road directions in the rural South, ours had been long on things like "the tall oak off to your left" and "the feeder barn set back from the road on the right" and "the double gates about a half mile past the watermelon patch," none of which were visible in the dense early morning haze.

Adding to the problem was a thick fog in my head that had not crept in on little cat feet—but I get ahead of myself.

This whole thing started in Tujague's bar on Decatur Street in New Orleans. I had stopped in with a friend to meet his cousin O.B. and O.B.'s friend Allen, who were up from Ft. Lauderdale for the Sugar Bowl. The topics of conversation were pretty wide-ranging, helped along by the ministrations of the ever-solicitous Forrest "Bartender to the Stars"

Mathern, but my attention narrowed when Friend Allen
brought up the subject of hunting wild boars, in Florida no
less. I didn't even know they existed there, and said so.

"Shit, man," he said, "they're all over. They're a damn
nuisance in a lot of places."

"What kind of guns," I asked, "do you hunt them with?"

"People are always asking me that and you know what
I tell them? Guns are for chickenshits! I hate guns. They're
only good for accidentally shooting one of your balls off."

He knew, and I knew, that he had his hook set in me pretty
good at this point, but I didn't mind playing straight man.

"Well, how do you hunt them?"

"We use dogs to run them down, then we grab them and
hogtie their ass."

I could see where this was heading, but I asked anyway.

"What kind of dogs do you use?"

"Use cur dogs, y'know, mixed breeds, as what we call
chase dogs, and pit bulls for the catch dog."

"And when do you hunt these wild boars?"

"Any goddamn time we want to."

"Would you take me with you sometime?"

In answer, Friend Allen wrote two telephone numbers
on a cocktail napkin and said to give him two weeks' notice
so he could set things up.

The rigors of freelance writing being what they are—trust me, they're elaborate, and chief among them is the anxiety over whether you'll ever get a piece finished, coupled with the anxiety over whether you'll ever get paid for it—it took me a good while to get around to calling Friend Allen. It was another good while before I actually got him on the phone. Even then, there was a pretty damn fair amount of calling back and forth before we could settle on a date for the hunt, but we did and I told him I'd call for directions to his place when I got to Florida.

Two weeks later I arrived in Tampa, where I looked forward to stuffing myself on authentic, tear-inducing barbecued ribs (something you can't find in New Orleans) at Big John's Alabama Barbecue on a funky stretch of 40th Street not far from Busch Gardens. Having fulfilled this spiritual need, I planned to take a leisurely, scenic drive down the west coast of Florida to Naples and cut across the Everglades Parkway, better known as Alligator Alley, to Ft. Lauderdale to hook up with Friend Allen.

I got a little panicky, however, when I couldn't reach him by phone. It dawned on me that if I had been told his last name those long months back at Tujaque's, I'd never written it down and had no earthly idea what it was. Several more calls proved fruitless, so I escaped into a fitful sleep.

The next morning, to my relief, he answered on the fifth ring. A slight feeling of unease returned, however, when in the space of a few minutes I learned that not only did I not really know who I was going to meet, I didn't know where the hell I was going. Friend Allen, it turned out, didn't live in Ft. Lauderdale, but near the small, unincorporated town of Immokalee, just northwest of the Everglades, thirty-five miles inland from Ft. Myers. Or more precisely, about smack dab in the middle of nowhere.

When I rolled into the place late that afternoon, I felt like I had made a wrong turn leaving Florida's west coast into a time/space warp and was entering a Central American border town. The narrow road was lined with one-room cantinas, taquerias, and cheap clothing stores whose signs were all in Spanish. Señoras with their babies milled about on the sidewalks. Here and there groups of Latin men stood talking in the shade of the storefronts, wearing khaki work clothes and the kind of *campesino* straw hats that are ubiquitous in Mexico, Honduras, or Salvador. Stout fellows, with the distinct Mayan features of Guatemala, shuffled up dust along the roadside. Down one stretch, for added cultural spice, there was a set of harsh looking two-story concrete barracks, the walkways and the courtyard between them filled with Haitians.

These people were the backbone of Immokalee, the migrant workers who pick the citrus, tomatoes, and other produce grown on the massive farms in this part of south Florida. It being Friday, payday, many of them were heading for the same place I was, Miner's Super Market, where I was to meet Friend Allen, who happened to own the place.

Miner's was at the far south end of town. With two gas pumps out front, it not only served as a one-stop *mercado*, but since most of the workers lacked a bank account, and in many cases writing skills, it was the place where they turned their paychecks into cash. Over a hundred were lined up from the entrance out into the parking lot when I pulled in.

Friend Allen, a big blond sun-weathered bear of a man, greeted me with a knuckle-popping handshake and a slap on the back and gave me a tour of his store.

The weekend specials included things like a five-pound bag of Maseca Instant Corn Masa Mix (*"para hacer: tortillas, tamales y otre platillos Mexicanos"*) or a four-pound bag of dried pinto beans for $1.99, fresh pig tails for sixty-nine cents a pound, and fresh neck bones and pig ears at two pounds for $1.00. There was an array of hot sauces that would have had mouths (and eyes) watering in deepest Cajun country. Surplus cotton/polyester work shirts for $2.99 came with name patches for Tom, Joe, and Bill already affixed.

Standing in front of the three checkout lines, he proudly pointed out a row of ten taxidermied wild boar heads mounted on the wall above the front doors. "Damned fine, aren't they?" he said. "I've got two more back in the freezer I haven't had time to get stuffed yet. Want to take one home with you?"

"Well," I stammered, "let me think about that one."

"I used to have a stuffed fourteen-foot, 500-pound alligator—Willie is his name—hanging from the ceiling over the frozen food section, but I took him home a while back. Got him hanging in my living room."

"Broke a lot of people's hearts around here, when he took him home," one of the cashiers informed me. "Folks from miles around used to come in just to see Willie."

"Listen," Friend Allen said, "grab a cold beer and sit with me while I cash a few hundred more paychecks. When I'm finished, we'll go out to the lake house and I'll take you out on the airboat. You'll love it."

Those were the most fateful words I heard all weekend. After hog hunting, the second favorite recreation for the men in Friend Allen's circle was to tear around nearby Lake

Trafford in their airplane-engine-powered airboats, just like the ones Marlin Perkins used to traverse the Everglades on *Wild Kingdom*.

By eight o'clock that evening, a crew of locals had gathered for the night's run. (They'd all seen wild hogs before, but never a writer so close up, so I seemed to be the main attraction for them.) There were four airboats in all, each one carrying the largest Igloo cooler you can buy, loaded with beer and stronger potables. The routine was to race one another for a while, terrorizing the hundreds of alligators whose eyes shone like a carpet of large red fireflies across the surface of the lake and the flocks of small coots, dumb orange-headed ducks who have to flap their wings and paddle their feet in the water for fifty yards before they can get airborne. Then everyone would pull into a slough for refreshments.

As the night wore on, the stops became more frequent and lasted longer than the racing around. Fellowship and conversation came to the fore, boat talk, fish talk, hog talk, drugs and '60s talk, talk about tours of duty in Vietnam, football, hell-raising drunken sprees, wives and ex-wives and girlfriends, wrecking cars, you name it. All well lubricated, of course, and all in all more uplifting than any number of "warrior weekends" the male movement honchos could put together in Marin County or the wilds of Omaha.

The downside, however, was on the level of snake shit in a wagon rut. By the time we had abandoned our male bonding and crawled into bed, it was four o'clock in the morning.

When Friend Allen shook me awake two hours later, I shot up in the bed, speaking in a tongue neither one of us had ever heard before. I couldn't focus my eyes, my temples pounded, and my tongue felt like someone had been using it for a razor strop. I was, however, fully dressed, down to my still laced Reeboks. I vaguely remember stumbling behind Friend Allen to his Ford Bronco and driving to his store, where we replenished the cooler with ice and beer and food for lunch, then headed for our hog hunting rendezvous. That stretch of time, though, is hazy and indistinct, clouded not so much by the fog that enveloped the land, as by the aforementioned thick fog in my head, into which I had almost fully escaped when Friend Allen slammed on his brakes, jammed the Bronco into reverse, and, making a wide arc, jolted to a stop beside Jose's red and white pickup. It was my second wake-up call of the day.

Jose leaned against the cab door of the truck grinning. In his mid to late forties, he was a second generation Mexican, who'd grown up in Immokalee and was the foreman on a local cattle ranch. Mexican George, a burly fireplug of a man in his thirties, had come to Florida from his home country a dozen years ago. He was Jose's chief *caballero* on the ranch and trained the dogs we would be using on the hunt. He, also, was grinning. It was obvious, from the jocular ribbing they gave us about our readiness to hunt hogs, that their preparation for the day had been far from the profligacy of our own.

The key to the treasure, like the man said, is the treasure. So we stood around waiting for Hayden (a recent graduate of the University of Georgia, who to his credit never once asked me "How 'bout them Dawgs?"). He had the key to the lock on the gate of the 13,000-acre farm we were parked in front of and the permission to scour those acres for wild hogs.

As we waited, Mexican George, who spoke in a soft, slow drawl, reminiscent of the lazy cousin of cartoon star Speedy Gonzalez, introduced me to the dogs. Crowded into the caged-in bed of the pickup were Maxie, a brown and black brindled pit bull; Pepe, a younger and smaller version of Maxie; Yella, his name the local pronunciation of the color yellow (as in "Yeller, Ol'"); Rambo, a lemon and white cur, who looked to have some bird dog blood; and Junior, who looked more like Ol' Yeller than Yella did. They were still and quiet in their cramped quarters, but they gave off an anticipatory tension as their eyes scanned the scrubland around them through the lifting fog, their nostrils flaring in the shifting breeze.

Just after eight o'clock, Hayden pulled up. He was late, but who were we to quibble? His eyes were lightly rimmed in red and he sported several days' growth of beard. He seemed to be an adherent of the Friend Allen school of training.

"We hunted all day yesterday," he said hoarsely, after nodding a perfunctory hello, "and my dogs got pretty cut up. I got them on penicillin and rest therapy, so I only brought Roscoe with me today, in case none of these other dogs can put the catch on a hog. Roscoe will catch anything. From forty pounds to 400."

Roscoe was the picture of repose, lying calmly in his cage with his chin resting on his forepaws. He was a compact black, white, and brown pit bull, who would maybe go seventy pounds, but he looked like one solid hunk of muscle, with a head bigger than my own and a set of jaws that gave me no doubt that Hayden's claim was true. His deep brown eyes seemed to look directly into my soul, and I quietly prayed that whatever he found there was to his liking.

Hayden opened the gate and we drove to a small stand of pines where his swamp buggy was parked. It was a custom made job, resembling a large Jeep, with a spare frame and a steel mesh floorboard, two bucket seats in front, and a large bench-like seat in back. Powered by a four-cylinder engine, it had four-wheel drive and was mounted on four-foot-tall tractor tires. There was no windshield and no shock absorbers. Two dog cages had been welded onto the rear end, and Hayden transferred Roscoe from his truck into one of them. Friend Allen got in the pickup with Jose and Mexican George. I climbed into the buggy with Hayden and we drove on deeper into the farm.

After about a mile, Hayden stopped next to a palmetto rush, a patch of the small palms that stretched off into the distance. Hogs, he allowed, liked to lay up in the shade of the palmetto fronds, so it was a good spot to loose the dogs. They hit the ground running, with Mexican George trailing them on foot, while the rest of us waited in the vehicles. The dogs are trained to keep silent until they roust a hog, so we would let them get out of sight for a quarter hour or so, then catch up with them. We spent the entire morning leapfrogging in this manner, running across tracks here and there and patches of upturned earth, looking like they had been hand-turned with a roto-tiller, where hogs had been rooting for food. But by midday, neither yelp of dog had been heard nor wild hog seen, so we drove back to our base camp for a lunch break.

Mexican George cut some palmetto fronds and made a pallet for himself in the shade, where he lay drinking Diet Coke and munching homemade stuffed tortillas. The rest of us tore open the packages of fried chicken laden with sliced jalapenos we had bought at Miner's Super Market and fished icy beers from the coolers. Though we were hot, some of us still a little green around the gills from lack of sleep, and we didn't have the first hog to show for a half-day's trouble, our spirits remained relatively high. Before long, I was being initiated into one of the auxiliary pleasures of hog hunting: telling hog stories.

"Hogs aren't indigenous to the Americas," Hayden volunteered.

"Where'd they come from?"

"Nearest anyone can figure, Columbus brought them to Cuba on his second voyage in 1493. De Soto brought huge droves of feral swine to feed his troops during his expeditions in the early 1500s and the hogs around here are descendents of that stock."

"A lot of farmers in this area release pure-bred sows into the wild herds to upgrade them," Jose chimed in.

"Whatever," Friend Allen said solemnly, shaking his head, "those sumbitches are mean. I've had 'em chase me up onto my swamp buggy more than once."

"Hell, yeah," said Hayden, "I've had them chase me in my pickup, trying to puncture my tires with their tusks."

"They bad, all right," said Jose. "Friend of mine ran up on a hog that must have weighed 268 pounds. He shot it with his .44 Magnum pistol. All four legs went out from under the hog and he slammed into the ground. I want you to know that damn hog got up and he had to shoot him two more times to put him down for good."

"The worst one I ever come up against," drawled Mexican George from his palmetto pallet, "was so bad I had to shoot him nine times with a .22 Magnum before I killed it."

"Well, that's all hogs," Jose said, "but nothing will beat the time George lassoed that wildcat."

Now the only thing I know about wildcats, outside of books and the Discovery Channel, is when I was a kid and my father used to take me fishing at Lake Grenada in north central Mississippi. We always stopped for breakfast at a cafe near the lake, where the owner had a wildcat in a cage in front of his place. It was a natural draw, and there was generally a group of men and boys standing around gawking at the creature. The cat, as I remember, was either lying quietly or idly pacing the cage, when KABOOM, out of nowhere, yowling like a banshee, he would explode head first into the heavy gauge steel wire of the cage like something shot out of a cannon, sending a major "lurky"—a rush of cold shit to the heart—through the crowd of scattering onlookers.

"Y'all are some lying sons of bitches," I said. And meant it.

"No, man," Mexican George drawled calmly from the shade. "Is true."

"Some kids came running up to my place," Jose continued, "yelling that George had a wildcat up a tree. I jumped in my pickup and when I got down to his place, I saw him up in one tree with a rope around the wildcat in another tree. By the time I stopped and got out, both of them were on the ground and George had that damn cat's legs tied up."

"George," I said, surrendering to the moment, "how the hell do you hogtie a goddamn wildcat?"

"Fast, man. You got to be real fast."

By the time we had hooted and laughed ourselves out, we were ready to resume the hunt. We drove to a far section of the farm we hadn't covered in the morning, and again Mexican George set out on foot with the dogs, while the rest of us resumed our start and stop following. After a couple of hours, I began to feel the day would boil down to a long ride around the south Florida landscape, which was pleasant enough as long as the beer held out. Hayden had told me he caught four hogs on the day before and Friend Allen had regaled me with tales of past hunts in which great numbers of the beasts had been bagged, seventeen in one day being the most. I was beginning to feel, however, that the prey we were after was as mythical as those of the boar hunts of Erymanthos or Kalydon I had read about in Greek legend.

I had, in fact, rather resignedly cracked a cold beer when we heard the dogs start baying, which meant the chase was on. I slammed my beer into a slot specifically designed for that purpose, as Hayden gunned the buggy toward the sound of the dogs.

We rounded the edge of a patch of saw grass and saw a large black boar bounding across an open swath of ground and into a marsh, the dogs in hot pursuit and Mexican George splashing behind them, up to his armpits in water.

"It looks like a bar hog," Hayden yelled over the engine roar. "Looks like his tail's been cut."

I had no idea what he was talking about, but I learned later that when these guys catch a boar, they castrate it and release it, after bobbing its tail. Often a hunter will make a personal marking of some kind (Hayden uses a notch in the left ear) to tell if a hog is "theirs" when caught again. This castrated boar is called a bar hog (no one could tell me where this name came from, so I was left to surmise a boar sadly releasing its "o" at the loss of his balls). Without the desire to chase sows, the bar hogs get fat and their meat is less gamey and more tender when they're slaughtered.

The marsh was too deep for his buggy to cross, so Hayden skirted its perimeter and cut the engine at a thicket on the far side. The buggy was still rolling forward when he hit the ground and plunged into the tangled brush, with me right behind him. We emerged into a small clearing, where the winded boar had decided to make his stand. Wild hogs cannot swivel their heads on their necks as humans can, so they have to plant their front feet and thrash their entire upper body from side to side to make effective use of their cutters, the long knife-like tusks that jut out at a slight angle from their lower jaw. They have a gnarly set of upper tusks called whetters, because they act as a whetstone for the lower tusks. To maintain the sharpness of his cutters, the boar continually snaps his jaws together, producing a sound like two pool balls colliding. This cracking, combined with the snorting grunts of the boar and the yapping and snarling of the dogs, was the soundtrack for the tableau we burst into.

The boar had stopped to battle Pepe, Maxie, and Junior, who were circling and making snapping lunges at it. Junior took a minor tusk cut and was sent rolling from the blow, but when the boar turned his attention to Maxie, Junior rushed in again, set his teeth into the hog's tough hide just behind its right ear, and laid in close to its body to stay clear of the slashing cutters. Do what he could, the boar couldn't shake Junior's hold.

Mexican George, an already noosed length of rope in his right hand, rushed the preoccupied hog and grabbed its hind legs. ("You can work 'em like a wheelbarrow," he told me afterwards, "when you got 'em like that.") He called Junior off the hog. With a heavy grunt, he twisted the hog onto its left side and in the same motion came down on it with his left knee lodged in the crook of its neck, pinning its head to the ground to neutralize tusk action. In a quick movement, he looped the noose around the boar's rear legs, tightened it, and then secured the front legs. Hogtied. As fine a job as you're ever likely to see.

The dogs lay stretched out in the grass, panting in canine self-satisfaction, as Hayden checked out the boar and found that he was, indeed, a bar hog, a keeper. After pulling the swamp buggy around, he and Mexican George, with great effort, manhandled the 180-pound hog into one of the dog cages.

"What will you do with him now?" I asked.

"I'll pen him up for a couple of months and feed him on

sweet corn," Hayden answered. "That'll clean him out and put some more weight on him before he goes to the meat market. Those will be the best two months of his life. That last day, though, that will definitely be his worst."

As we remounted the swamp buggy and I spied my beer, hot now and half-empty from the jouncing of the chase, I felt a kinship with the Arkadian Ankaios. If you remember your Greek legends, you know he was about to enjoy some wine from his new vineyards when his soothsayer came forth with the famous adage, "Much lies between the cup and the edge of the lip."

A cry went up that a wild boar was rooting up his grapes, at which point he set down his untasted wine, rushed off in a bearskin with a double axe, and met his death at the tusks of the Kalydonian boar. Opening a fresh beer, I took solace in the fact that my encounter with the Immokaleean boar had not been so dire.

We set out again after a short rest, but I don't think anyone's heart was in it except Hayden, the youngest in the group. By five o'clock the dogs hadn't run up another hog, so we all gathered in the shade of a small stand of pines to talk things over. There was still plenty of sunlight and the heat had subsided some and Hayden was ready to hunt 'til dark or after.

None of the others would say they were ready to quit outright. They looked to me, the guest, the greenhorn, for a yea or a nay. It was, indeed, less hot than it had been since seven that morning, but my earlobes were the consistency of fried pork rinds, the adrenaline I'd been running on all day was pretty much depleted by the capture of the boar (probably the only one I'd ever witness in this lifetime), and beyond that I was leaving the next morning. My answer came easy to me. When I said, "Fellas, I think I've had all I can stand for one day," I thought I saw a veiled gratefulness pass over the faces of Jose, Mexican George, and Friend Allen. Even the dogs.

Hayden took it in stride, though I could tell my stock had gone down in his estimation. While Mexican George loaded his dogs, Hayden quietly picked up an empty beer can from the floorboard, took out his Buck knife, and stuck it into the can, carefully cutting in a circle until he had taken off the top two inches. Filling this makeshift cup with ice from the cooler, he pulled a bottle of bourbon from his knapsack and poured himself a healthy dollop.

"On our way out," he said, after silently sipping his sour mash for a few minutes, "let's run back by that canal on the far side of the squash patch. There's a big-ass gator must go at least fourteen feet that's been laying up around there lately."

"Yeah, man," Mexican George drawled from his perch on top of the dog cages, "lez go and lasso him."

BAYED SOLID

"Awesome," my new friend Jimbo says *sotto voce.* "Intense. Vibrant."

He is describing, believe it or not, a mixed breed dog named Alabama, a smaller version of Ol' Yeller, who is in the bay pen at the 6th Annual Uncle Earl's Hog Dog Trials, trying to "control" a 350-pound feral pig.

Jimbo has taken me under his wing, and over a long hot weekend at the Winn Parish Fairgrounds, he has been educating me in the finer points of judging hog dogs. (There is a reason for everything, a friend once told me, but not always a normal reason, and I think that applies here.)

"Good cadence," Jimbo says. "And real good slobber! Look at it fly!"

Slobber, you see, is good. Very good. It means the dog is holding nothing back, giving (the always elusive and laudable) 110 percent, leaving it all on the field. Well, the bay pen in this instance. You could almost say that slobber is one of the "intangibles" of a good hog dog, except for the fact that unlike Gertrude Stein's Oakland there is so much *there* there.

"It's possible for a dog to get a perfect score without a lot of slobber," Jimbo says, "but all other things being equal, it is definitely going to come in second to a dog that's really letting it loose."

I don't think I'll ever forget that.

Uncle Earl's Hog Dog Trials are named in honor of Earl K. Long and were inaugurated in 1995, on the 100th anniversary of his birth. "Uncle" Earl was the most colorful and well-liked governor Louisiana has ever elected, which is saying a mouthful. He and his more (in)famous brother Huey P. Long (at least he was until Paul Newman played Earl in the movie *Blaze*) came from the nearby town of Winnfield. Unlike Huey, who seemed to hunger only for power (every man a king, indeed, starting with him), Earl K. often had a hankering for some sugar-cured wild hog meat with his morning eggs and grits, before he started showing everybody who was boss. He liked to hunt and kill his own hogs so much, the trials were a natural tribute to his memory.

The organizers of Uncle Earl's (to use the familiar diminutive) say it is the largest event of its kind in the world, and

I, for one, take them at their word. The record attendance
is the 3,500 folks who showed up in year two of the trials,
and while the crowds this year didn't match the record, in
my estimation it wasn't missed by much. An awful lot of
people were there, with an awful lot of dogs—Catahoula
hounds, Plott hounds, treeing Walkers, mountain and black
mouth and Florida cracker curs, and a passel of mixed breed
curs that have the blood of any or all of the aforementioned,
plus bird dog and bulldog, and I don't know what else.
From the sound of them, it seemed like dogs outnumbered
humans.

Webster tells us that the intransitive verb "bay" means
"to bark excitedly and continually," and I cannot stress hard
enough that last word, "continually." For four long days
and nights, the air at the fairgrounds was filled with the
baying of hundreds upon hundreds of hog dogs from all
over the country. Approximately 600 of them would compete against each other for the title of "Best of the Best" and
a seven-foot-tall trophy. The rest were there to be shown
off, traded, sold, or simply to keep their owners company.

Whenever I had mentioned to someone that I was going
up to Uncle Earl's, to a person they had two immediate

questions: What is a hog dog? and What are hog dog trials? The first question was easy. Hog dogs, also called bay dogs, hunt wild hogs. More specifically, they chase them down and corner them—keep them "at bay"—until their owners arrive on the scene and decide whether or not they want to "take" the hog. (I believe this last speaks for itself.) The second question was more problematic, as I had never attended any hog dog trials. The answer I settled on was that they were kind of like a hog and dog rodeo, which seemed to satisfy everyone, and as it turned out, was pretty close to the truth.

The bay pen at Uncle Earl's is a regulation rodeo arena that has been cut in half with a temporary fence that serves as the eastern boundary. Bleachers stand just outside the north and south fences. The hogs, captured in the wild by local hunters who use them for training their own dogs and for dog trials, are released into the bay pen, in their turn, through a large wooden gate in the middle of the western wall. Above this gate is a raised and covered plat-form where the five judges for the trials sit.

After the hog has had a little time to limber up, an owner brings his dog into the bay pen on leash. When he releases it, the dog has two minutes to show its stuff before the time-keeper blows his whistle. Of course, the hogs have a say in how good or bad a dog's stuff adds up. Some hogs just sidle up the fence, or head to a corner of the arena, and refuse to budge. Others are full of piss and vinegar, refusing to be cornered, charging again and again at the dogs, occasionally getting their snouts and tusks under a dog and tossing it into the air like a stuffed toy.

Judging bay dogs is a very complex thing, not something you pick up in a weekend, even with a knowledgeable mentor like Jimbo. The simplest explanation is that dogs are judged on how low they are to the ground when working the hog; their closeness to the hog; the constancy (the cadence) of their baying; their discipline and concentration; and most importantly, their ability to control and contain the hog without injuring it—if a dog bites a hog and holds on to it for longer than five seconds, it is disqualified. End of story, hit the showers, better luck next time.

Thirty points is a perfect score. (Don't ask.)

Every dog that receives a perfect score in the prelims is eligible for the Best of the Best Bay Off. Owners pay a $200 entry fee that goes into a winner-takes-all pot. Twenty-four dogs started the bay off; all of them damn fine hog dogs. Out of that twenty-four came fifteen. Out of fifteen, five

moved to the next level. Three dogs, one out of Georgia
and two from Texas, made the finals: Billy Long's Bubba,
Randall Wiggins' Coushatta, and Robbie Nugent's Useless.

Bubba was a four-time winner at Uncle Earl's, but Jimbo
and I had felt he was off his championship form all day. He
didn't do anything you could deduct points for, but he got
a soft 30 on our scorecard for lack of intensity and swing-
ing too wide as he worked the hog.

Jimbo was partial to Useless because his owner was a
friend. The dog had been fantastic all day, but his bay for
the gold was not his best performance. He got another soft
30, but we gave him the edge on Bubba.

Coushatta, however, a feisty little mixed cur out of Texas,
made such hair splitting unnecessary, by turning in a performance that a blind man would have known was perfect. He moved in on the hog immediately and went nose
to nose with it, his chin practically touching the ground.
His eyes never left the hog. His cadence was like a metro-
nome, and his front paws stabbed the ground in perfect
time with each bay. That hog tried over and over again to
escape, but it could not move from the spot where Coushatta held it. The cur had it bayed solid. As good as it gets.

And yes, slobber was flying with every bay. You know it
was. There was actually a terrible beauty to it, thin ropes

of slobber hanging for a moment in midair, suspended in time, sparkling in the sunlight like a nimbus around the heads of dog and hog.

MULLETHEADS

John from Odenville, Alabama, was mugging for the camera, arms spread, a mullet stuffed headfirst into his mouth.

This was my introduction to the 13th Annual Interstate Mullet Toss at the legendary Flora-Bama Lounge, which sits astride the Alabama-Florida state line. The Flora-Bama opened in 1962 as a small roadhouse and package store, but it is now a honky-tonk empire, open 365 days a year, that consists of a 100-foot beachfront, three live music stages, an oyster bar, a limousine service, a recording studio, and ten— count 'em, ten!—full-service bars.

Lightning crackled out over the Gulf of Mexico, thunder rolled in with the waves, and tropical rain beat down steadily. It did not seem to me a propitious day for the throwing of mullet.

John from Odenville, however, set me straight, exclaiming to anyone within earshot, "When you throwing mullet, dammit, it's rain or shine!"

Thirteen years ago, Flora-Bama owner Joe Gilchrist was trying to come up with an idea to beef up his business in the
early spring. His friend Jimmy Louis, a musician and song-
writer, suggested a contest in which people would compete
to see how far they could toss a mullet from Florida into
Alabama. Gilchrist, a laid-back sort of guy, thought, "Why
not?"

From this simple and wacky start, the Mullet Toss has
turned into an annual festival that draws more than 60,000
people over three days. Most come simply to party, but
almost 1,200 people sign up for the Mullet Toss.

Why do they do it? I don't know. The mullet is said to
possess mystical properties. I repeat this exactly as it was
presented to me, without further elaboration or explanation. I just don't know. The phenomenon is simply ineffa-
ble. Put out a barrel of mullet, and someone will come to
throw one.

Mullet used in the Toss weigh approximately a pound and
are a little over a foot long. (And in answer to the single
most-often asked question I get when telling people about
mullet tossing: Yes, they are dead.) They are tossed from a
ten-foot throwing circle on the Florida side of the state line

down a fifty-foot-wide rectangular "alley" that stretches 200 feet into Alabama. The sideline boundaries and twenty-five-foot sections the length of the alley are marked off with orange tape.

"We are burdened with so many rules in this life," Joe Gilchrist explained to me, "mostly by the government, that we try to keep them to a minimum at the Toss."

The rules are indeed few and reasonable. You may kiss your mullet, but you cannot pour beer into it. If you step out of the throwing circle during your throw or follow-through, you are disqualified, and the same goes for throwing your fish out of bounds. You can't use gloves. The mullet must be sand-free. And you must retrieve your own mullet and deposit it in the designated water bucket (the mullet are recycled). You get only one qualifying throw.

There are several tossing styles. One can grasp the mullet by the tail and toss it overhand, underhand, or sidearm. (This style is looked down upon by veteran tossers because, they say, the mullet will slip too easily out of your hand.) There is the football-style toss, which is self-explanatory. Joe Gilchrist demonstrated his "airplane" technique of tossing, explaining how you must adjust the side fins just so to get proper aerodynamics, etcetera, but I don't think any serious tosser would put much faith in this method.

John from Odenville, who was making his maiden toss, had an interesting tossing style, holding the mullet by its tail, spinning like a discus thrower, and releasing in the middle of the third spin. I wouldn't recommend this method. It looked good, but John didn't make the cut.

Far and away, the most popular and most effective tossing style was the "baseball" or "meatball" style. The mullet is folded (as nearly as possible) in half, with the tail on top, gripped with the fingers with head forward, and held firmly with the thumb. The release is as if you were throwing a baseball in from deep center field.

Qualifying takes place over two days, and the six contestants in each category recording the longest distances meet in the championship finals. There are fifteen categories in the competition for men and women, grouped by age, from ages one through seven to seventy plus.

Mullet tossing, however, is a young man's game. Most of the attention is on the twenty-one through thirty-nine men's division, where the longest distances are attained and the records set.

The record distance in the Mullet Toss is 178 feet and is held by twenty-six-year-old Michael "Woody" Bruhn, a fire-protection system installer from Spring Hill, Tennessee, a small town south of Nashville. Woody (his nickname comes from the fact that he is the spitting image of the actor Woody Harrelson) not only holds the world record for mullet tossing, he has also been the champion of the Mullet Toss for the past three years.

"I really can't say in so many words," Woody told me, when I asked what had drawn him to mullet tossing. "I was down here on vacation five years ago. I didn't throw that year, but I saw all the pictures of the Mullet Toss on the Flora-Bama's walls, and when I got back home I just decided I had to have my picture up there too. So I've been here every year since, and been lucky enough to have won the thing three years in a row. It just came naturally to me."

Woody, of course, uses the baseball tossing method, but he does no special training other than "just drink a few beers and keep my arm loose."

In his qualifying throw on Saturday, Woody showed he was the man to beat, with a distance of 178 feet 3 inches.

On Sunday, the weather cleared and a huge crowd was on hand for the finals. I found Woody watching the last of the qualifiers, sipping a beer.

"They say there's a guy out here with a pretty good arm," he told me, "but I haven't seen him throw yet."

Not that he seemed worried, but I pointed out nobody had tossed anywhere near his 178 feet 3 inches.

"I won't throw that far today," Woody said. "There's no rain, but the wind is way stronger than yesterday."

The three finalists up before Woody tossed 98 feet, 127 feet 8 inches, and 123 feet, respectively. Woody positioned his mullet to his satisfaction and windmilled his throwing arm a few times. He got a fine toss, but at 146 feet 6 inches, it was not up to championship record form.

He was, however, now four-time Champion of the Interstate Mullet Toss, and we chatted briefly as he collected his prizes: a hand-painted mullet plaque, a big plastic Miller Lite battery-operated wall clock, and a $50 bar tab at the Flora-Bama.

"I don't think I'm gonna toss next year," Woody confided to me as he accepted congratulations from his peers.

"Why not?" I asked.

"When you're in competition," he said, with a big *Cheers*-y grin, "you have to stay too sober."

SHOTGUN GOLF

It was barely past seven in the morning and the north Alabama hills were alive—but not with the sound of music. As I crossed the pasture toward the Pine Ridge Sporting Clays clubhouse, the tune echoing through the thickets and hollows of St. Clair County was being played with a variety of 410-, 20-, and 12-gauge shotguns.

What it was, was shotgun golf. The shooting of sporting clay targets on a number of "fields" scientifically laid out like holes on a golf course. "The ultimate simulated shotgun hunting sport for all seasons," according to brochures, and one of the fastest growing pastimes in the country.

The sport evolved out of trap and skeet shooting in the 1920s in England, where, presumably, a certain portion of the population was so chafed from the burden of Empiredom that they desperately needed something new and different to fill their leisure time.

Sporting clays began to catch on here in the 1980s and proved so addictive that the National Sporting Clays Association was formed in 1989. Headquartered in San Antonio, Texas, the NSCA now boasts of 12,000 members in 400 clubs across the country; publishes a monthly magazine, *Sporting Clays*; and hosts an annual National Championship tournament.

To my chagrin, I was aware of none of this when my old friend Lockjaw (a nickname he earned from his penchant for drinking shots of Jägermeister until his jaws clench up so bad he has trouble finishing sentences) invited me up to Pine Ridge to try out the sporting clays course he had just opened.

"You'll love it," he told me. "It has everything. Beautiful scenery, fresh air, light exercise, hand-eye coordination. It's competitive. You keep score—Xs for hits, Os for misses. It's inexpensive—$15 a round plus your shells. Kids are good at it. And women. Even people in wheelchairs can participate in this sport. You can't beat it for honing your wing shooting skills. Plus, there's nothing like the smell of gunpowder early in the morning."

All commendable attributes, of course, but honing my wing shooting skills has never been high on my priority list. In fact, it is rarely these days that I think of shooting anything—outside the poor cracked-out bastard who snatched my wife's purse right at our front door a couple of months ago, or New Orleans motorists who, with maddening regularity, make left turns from the right lane with no warning and no signal. But shotgun golf, the resonance of the phrase, somehow made traveling a long distance to humiliate myself seem a worthwhile endeavor.

Outfitted by Lockjaw in a baseball cap bearing the Pine Ridge logo, bright yellow safety goggles, and a canvas carpenter's apron holding two boxes of shotgun shells, I stepped into the shooter's stand on the first field.

The "course" at Pine Ridge consists of eight fields spread over twelve acres. Each field has a name—Decoying Woodies, E-Z Teal, Flushing Quail—that describes the shooting experience you will have there. A perfect score for one full round is 50.

The bright orange clay targets are the standard size used in trap and skeet: $4\,1/4$ inches in diameter and $1\,1/8$ inches thick. For a more difficult challenge, a shooter could choose a "midi" clay ($3\,1/2$ inches in diameter and $7/8$-inch thick) or a "mini" ($2\,3/8$ inches in diameter and $3/4$-inch thick). To keep you on your toes, occasionally the trap operator (the trapper) will throw a special white "poison bird" target, which represents an illegal species. If you pull the trigger on this one, you are automatically assessed a miss.

I, of course, was shooting at the largest clay available,

and setting in motion the ritual of sporting clays, I called out, "Shooter ready."

At that shout, the trapper yells back what target will be thrown—a single, a simultaneous pair, or a report pair (where the trapper releases the second clay at the blast of your first shot), followed by "Trapper ready."

Taking a deep breath, I shouted, "Pull!"

The metallic SLANG of the trap rang out and two orange disks floated out of the tree line from a slope above the shooting stand, like ducks descending to a lake. The 20-gauge jolted twice into my shoulder and in my mind's eye I saw orange clay shards exploding into the clear morning air. My real eyes, however, saw the targets fall unscathed to the ground, and my ears in the sudden quiet heard only the delicate sound of No. 8 birdshot falling on the underbrush. Though I managed to hit one of the six targets thrown, that rustling in the underbrush was a sound I was to become very familiar with.

The second field, E-Z Teal, simulated pairs of these small river ducks "springing up off a beaver pond." It was here that I encountered my first *battue*. Affectionately called "bad news battues," these black targets are the same size as a standard sporting clay, but only 3/8-inch thick. They are also flat, which means they explode out of the trap rather than spring and they do nothing but accelerate, even in their downward trajectory. I felt obliged to pull the trigger on my battue, but it was an empty gesture, as the damn thing was moving so fast I barely saw it. Five targets here, zero hits.

To my amazement, I scored two out of five on the Flushing Quail field, primarily because sporting clays move at a slower pace than the real thing. On Slippery Snipe, however, where the targets are thrown from behind you, I was back to form, hitting only one of five.

The Fur & Feather field was the most fun, mainly due to the "rabbit" target. A standard clay with a reinforced rim, this target speeds out of the trap and rolls across the field, executing "hops, leaps, and bounds that would make a real rabbit turn fuzzy with envy." (Who writes these brochures?) The extra challenge on this field was that a rabbit target would be immediately followed by a bird target, so you had to ground-sight the rabbit, shoot, and then swing back to take the bird on the wing, as it were. Score: two bunnies, no birds; two of eight.

I was dismal on the Trapper's Surprise field, where you stand on a platform built above the trap station. There were three lanes of fire: left, straight ahead, and to the right. Below me, the trapper could throw the targets into any lane he desired, and in any sequence. I came out on the short end of the guessing game, hitting one clay out of eight.

On Way-Out Dove, I was even worse. The trapper slung the targets in singles and pairs. They sailed high above the tallest of the pine trees that hugged the perimeter of the field and hung there silhouetted against the bright sky before disappearing untouched by my birdshot. I think I allowed myself to become distracted by a memory of gamey dark-roasted dove flesh, accompanied by a steaming mound of cheese grits, fresh asparagus, and a good cabernet—but I digress. Zip on this field.

My shining moment came on the last field of the course, White Wing. It was never made clear to me exactly what kind of feathered vertebrate this field was supposed to sim-ulate, but the targets came straight at me from a long dis-tance, allowing more than ample time to take a bead on them, and I had the extreme pleasure of blasting five out of six of the little orange fuckers into smithereens.

This one field had saved me from the ignominy of scor-ing in single digits. My final score was 10 out of 50. Twenty percent! Me, who had qualified as a Sharpshooter on the Marine Corps rifle range—missing Expert by the barest of points. It was degrading.

"There's been worse," Lockjaw told me. "Look at it this way. You can only get better."

There was truth in what he said, and I'll admit there was a voice inside me urging me to have another go at it, to redeem myself. I resisted, however. Hell, it was just a game really, but not my game.

I could see, though, that Lockjaw might be right about the sport being the coming thing. You can indulge yourself with some nifty gear—shotguns, message caps, safety goggles or high-tech high-end sunglasses, shooting gloves, camouflage clothes, leather shell pouches—which turns a lot of people on. You keep score and you can shoot in groups, so that opens the door for some side wagering to take place, which always spices up sporting activities.

But the main allure, in my opinion, is that it is perfect for the sensitive guy who likes the outdoors, male bonding, and shooting guns, but doesn't want to kill anything. Sort of like a photo safari, but noisier.

"You could put it that way, I reckon," Lockjaw told me when I voiced this feeling, "but for most of these guys, sporting clays are just something ELSE to kill."

BARBWIRE:
Postcards from the Edge
of NASCAR'S Infield

It's a long haul from Thunder Road to Speedway Boulevard in Charlotte, North Carolina. You can't measure it in miles.

The old moonshine runners, who, legend has it, took their daredevil driving skills into stock car racing to make some legitimate money, would surely be astounded at the grandeur of the Charlotte Motor Speedway and the hordes of people who show up there on the first weekend in October for a 500 mile race.

The Charlotte race is one of thirty-six in the Winston Cup Series, the heavyweight division of NASCAR, which begins each year in February at Daytona and ends at the Atlanta Motor Speedway in November. All NASCAR races have sponsors and this year Charlotte's is called the UAW-GM Quality 500.

But I did not go to Charlotte to see the race. I went to observe the "rhubarbs."

For several months, my friend John McDonald had been calling and urging me to come to a NASCAR event and hang out in the infield of the race track where fans he called "the rhubarbs" camped out for the long race weekend. "It's wild, man," was his reiterative exhortation.

John, a.k.a. Johnny Mack, a.k.a. the Deli Lama, has been a stage actor, a rockabilly singer, a restaurant manager, and a caterer on the rock concert and professional wrestling circuits. For the past few years, he has been crew chief for The Finish Line, a catering company that provides the eats and drinks to the racing swanks who lease box suites at a half dozen speedways around the country. But essentially, Johnny Mack is a disciple of, and an evangelist for, the gonzo way of life.

We go back thirty years and have been partners in a variety of escapades, many of which were dangerous, illegal, and involved moral turpitude. So I was a little wary of his invitation, not being as keen for Gonzo adventures as I once was. My old pal, however, finally wore me down.

Since most of John's calls had been post-midnight, after he got his mind right, it had taken awhile for it to dawn on me that these "rhubarbs" had not been referred to by that term until John invented it.

"I was up in a box suite one day with a couple of guys on my crew," he told me. "There was a classic car show down in the infield and I noticed this couple looking wistfully at one of those beautifully restored 1940s era cars. The wife was a very hefty bleached blonde, squeezed into a pair of short shorts. The guy was drinking a beer. He had on a ball cap and a patch of his beer belly was peeking out from the bottom of his t-shirt. He was pulling a little red wagon with a cooler of beer in it. I just shook my head and said to the boys, 'Man, look at those rhubarbs!'"

"How would you spell that?" I asked.

"Like the vegetable," John answered.

"I thought maybe it was 'rue'-barbs, because that couple couldn't afford a classic car," I said. "Or that it came from the root word 'rube'."

"Not really."

I began to feel I was in a situation similar to H. Allen Smith's when he was writing *The Rebel Yell*, in which he set out to discover the correct spelling of that "screech of the Confederate Soldier." Dadaist that he is, the word "rhubarb" lit up in John's brain, he spoke it, and that is all the meaning we are liable to find in it.

Well, with me boyo John being such a character, his personality so infectious, his manner of speaking so colorful and entertaining, the name stuck. Everyone he works with, from the top brass on down, began to talk about "rhubarbs." And everyone they have social intercourse with started using the word. And now I and the people I know do. And so on.

He didn't stop there though. For NASCAR fans higher on the economic ladder than rhubarbs, the folks who can afford Winnebago or Pace Arrow motor homes, or $200,000-plus American Eagle buses, he coined the term "nabobs" (pronounced NAY-bobs).

"Yeah man," John said, "you got your rhubarbs and your nabobs, and then the big dogs up in the box suites. I don't know what you'd call them."

Race week at a NASCAR event has an eerie beginning. On Tuesday, when the garbage barrels are put out on the acres and acres of campground that ring the speedway, a slow trickle of pickups and campers and RVs begins to arrive and set up camp on their rented plots. As the week progresses, the trickle becomes a flood, and by race day the speedway has become a small city of approximately 200,000 people.

The infield area is like the French Quarter of this city. It's where the action is. The drivers and their crews live there in their expensive motor homes. The garages that house the cars, the pit area, pit road, the media center, the hospital and its helipad, they're all there. And of course, so are the hardcore fans, the rhubarbs and nabobs alike who have come together not only to cheer for their favorite drivers, but to get down with some non-stop serious partying. For three or four days.

The track at Charlotte is a mile-and-a-half oval and the infield area has a network of asphalt and dirt roads that divide it into neighborhoods. The 'hood at the northwest end, by Turn 4, heading into the straightaway and the finish line, is the most upscale, where the nabobs stay. Over by Turn 3 is solidly middle- to upper middle-class. The Turn 1 area is middle class running to rhubarb, and Turn 2 is hardcore rhubarb.

I met a gnomish rhubarb with a Zapata moustache on Friday night in Turn 2. He was part of a foursome—along with Glenn from Spartanburg, and Bryant and Greg from Greensboro—pitching horseshoes in the light spilling from around the reflector boards used for night racing. My diminutive *bandolero* was very drunk, and he managed to maintain that condition all the way through Sunday. And Monday morning too, as far as I know.

"They say that the fans here on the second turn are the most obnoxious fans of all," he told me with some pride. "But I go back and forth from here over to the third turn. They're pretty rowdy over there too."

"Tomorrow night, ol' Bryant here," volunteered Greg, who turned out to be the talker of the bunch, "he's gonna dress up like Texas Pete and take him a promenade around to all the parties." (Texas Pete is a brand of hot sauce made in Winston-Salem, North Carolina, and the name of the image of a solid red cowboy wearing chaps and a ten-gallon hat and twirling a lariat on the label.)

I expressed interest in seeing such a thing.

"Oh yeah, it's way cool," Greg told me. "We had our picture in *National Geographic* one time!"

"Did you have clothes on?" I countered.

"Yeah, yeah. But they coulda got us nekkid if they'd wanted to!"

About that time, a pickup full of young people came slowly up the road. They were throwing something to the folks on the infield grass, like doubloons being thrown from a parade float at Mardi Gras. When I bent to see what they were tossing, I found they were Jell-O shots, in small plastic cups, tightly sealed with little plastic tops.

I dropped in on Bryant and his crew Saturday afternoon during the Busch Series All Pro Bumper-to-Bumper 300. *Poco Zapata* was basically incoherent, but standing, and it looked to me like Bryant would never make it to his promenade.

He fooled me though. When I ambled up to his truck around eight o'clock that night, Bryant was getting into his Texas Pete outfit: red cowboy boots, red jeans, red Western-style shirt, red bandana, a red ten-gallon hat he had made by jamming an inverted two-liter plastic bottle into the crown of a straw cowboy hat and molding a high dome around it with some kind of thin plastic. He donned a pair of red homemade chaps, and strapped on a red double-holstered gun belt with two red plastic shooting irons. He pulled on a pair of red gloves, and slung a lariat painted red over his shoulder. A girl applied red greasepaint to his face and ears and neck. He was, indeed, a living, breathing, inebriated Texas Pete.

Beer in hand, ol' Pete—I could never again call him by his given name—took off down the infield road, an entourage following in his wake, one of whom pulled a red wagon with an ice chest full of reloads. The night air resonated with his battle cries: "Ooooweeee! I'm hot!" "Ooooweee! It's gonna be a hot one tonight!" And the very best of all: "Just say NO! to Tabasco! Say YES! to Texas Pete!"

This was the third consecutive year Bryant has costumed as Texas Pete, and everywhere we went (which was everywhere in the infield) people called out to him, came over to shake his hand or slap him on the back, offered him a beer or a pull of whiskey, yelled at him to pull out his guns. (He would tell me later in the night, his hand on my shoulder to steady himself, his face close to mine, "I learned one thing tonight. I never knew I was so popular.")

I lost Pete at tony Turn 4, at the karaoke stage. One minute he was out in the crowd doing the Electric Slide, the next he was gone.

The karaoke stage—the best and biggest party of the night—was organized by Joe McKenzie and some of his pals. Joe is a homeboy, a sixty-two-year-old real estate broker in Charlotte, and he loves to party. "My wife Pat and I have gone to as many as twenty-two races a year," he boasted, "but we've cut back some."

Joe was the emcee at the fairly elaborate setup. There was a book listing all the songs that were on tape, and revelers could pick one and sign up to perform it. Two small, multicolored disco balls rotated on a pedestal on top of one of the JBL speakers mounted on tripod stands. Joe held court behind the stand-up microphone, wearing a billed cap with a glans penis for a crown. ("They'll let any dickhead be an emcee!") He introduced the singers and periodically directed the crowd into a line dance or the Macarena.

Joe and the gang showed no signs of slowing down at midnight, but I wanted to get down to the south end of the infield for the start of the wagon races. They took place on a rise everybody called Redneck Hill, the highest point in the infield, and consisted of very drunk grown men getting into kid-size little red wagons and letting as many very drunk friends as could get their hands on the racers' backs give them a running shove down the asphalt slope, cheered on by a very drunk and raucous crowd.

I guess the point of it all was to simply make it down the slope unharmed, and some of the racers attained that goal, although their number diminished as the night wore on. For the most part, the pushers turned the racers over before even reaching the incline of the road, or the racers collided with each other and spilled from their wagons, or individual racers turned their own wagons over and skidded across the asphalt. And this went on until security called a halt to it.

It was wild, man.

Oh yeah. Dale Jarrett won the UAW-GM Quality 500. It took over five hours to complete the race. There were eleven caution flags, and one red flag total stoppage that lasted almost an hour, because the sewer line out by Highway 29 backed up and overflowed from a drainage pipe onto the racetrack. There were six wrecks, one involving a dozen cars. All of them were on Turn 2.

I hooked back up with the Deli Lama on the first weekend in November for the Napa 500 at the Atlanta Motor Speedway (AMS), the final race of the Winston Cup Series, to see what kind of rhubarb craziness would transpire at that venue. The weather turned cold and rainy, which really put a damper on things, but despite that I have to say that the crowd at the AMS didn't hold its booze very well and was a bit on the surly side. The parties, if you could call them that, were small and clannish. That crowd could not hold a candle to the fans in Charlotte. It was lame, man.

Except, that is, for the party thrown by Stan from Daytona and Dr. Dave from Dayton, Ohio, whom I met Saturday afternoon while searching for Joe McKenzie's Tropic Cruiser. The interior of their large tent featured outdoor carpeting, ferns and other houseplants, easy chairs, a long table and a TV in the dining area, and a camp heater that kept things toasty. They were about to assemble the hot tub (!), and invited me to join them later in the evening.

When I returned, the first person I saw was Joe McKenzie, wearing his dickhead hat. "This is the best party you'll find down here," he told me. "I knew that," I replied, "when I saw you."

Dr. Dave's partner, Nurse Vickie, had laid out quite a spread. There were chunks of cantaloupe and honeydew melon wrapped in ham, a nice Brie, a vegetable tray, various dips with chips, sharp cheddar cubes with red and green grapes, and chocolate mousse balls by David Glass that she had ordered from Balducci's.

Dr. Dave mixed up his traditional batch of Purple Penises in a small plastic garbage can, a "secret" concoction that I know contained 151 rum, vodka, and curaçao. Everyone had to chug from Dr. Dave's Purple Penis Dispenser, and the rule was that it could never be set down until it was empty. Longtime nabob neighbors rotated in and out of the hot tub. And a grand time was had by all.

As for the Napa 500, it was worse than Charlotte. The race started at 12:40 p.m. and rain stoppages delayed it for over six hours. Of the 160,000 fans present for the start, less than half were around when the abbreviated race was completed near 11 p.m. Jeff Gordon, the driver fans love to hate, placed first, his thirteenth win of this season, tying a modern-era record set by King Richard Petty in 1975. He had already clinched the Winston Cup Championship for the third time in five years.

The morning after the race, several thousand rhubarbs lined up in the rain for the annual free "Breakfast of Champions." Johnny Mack and The Finish Line crew had been up all night preparing scrambled eggs, grits, sausage biscuits, regular biscuits, bacon, and link sausages.

A lonely Keebler Elf stood at the back of the overflow garage, wiggling his little fingers to no one, while Tony the Tiger was being mobbed over in the main garage. DJs from an Atlanta country-music station carried on the way they do. The tables that filled both garages were piled high with boxes of honey buns, Slam Dunks, pecan spins, minidonuts, cookies, Wheatables, and Cheez-Its. After Jeff Gordon made his brief, obligatory appearance, lines of rhubarbs filed out of the breakfast, toting all the cartons of freebies they could handle.

As I wandered on my way to the main kitchen to say goodbye to me wild John boyo, the Keebler Elf was still standing all alone, wiggling his little fingers.

When I told this to the Deli Lama, he looked me in the eyes and said, "Hell, man. You know them elves don't like to be touched."

HOLLERIN'

Spivey's Corner, North Carolina, does have a traffic light, which is more than can be said for Plain View, its western, and bigger, neighbor. It has several, actually, all at the same crossroads. It even has a marble monument: "Welcome To Spivey's Corner, Hollerin' Captial of the Universe."

Back in 1984, at the monument's unveiling, there was an awkward moment that is now legendary. A teacher attending the ceremony pointed out to Ermon Godwin, co-founder of the Annual National Hollerin' Contest, that the "t" and the "i" in "Capital" had been transposed. Mr. Godwin, to his credit, maintained his savoir faire, calmly telling the woman, "That's the way we pronounce it up here."

From this, you can see that people in these parts are very keen on phonology—or linguistic morphology, that may be closer to the point. They see a difference between hollering and hollerin' that is, for my taste, splitting the hair a mite thin.

JUNIOR! IF YOU DON'T GET DOWN OUT OF THAT

TREE, I'M GOING TO TAN YOUR HIDE! Now that, I would call yelling, but I can see how folks could consider it to be hollering, as opposed to hollerin'. I can now.

It's complicated.

So, let's let hollering lie for the time being, and focus our attention on hollerin'. Which is a hard thing NOT to do at the National Hollerin' Contest, where a varied assortment of folks are letting loose with sounds that will carry a good four miles, maybe farther, bouncing off stands of pine windbreaks along their way.

Hollerin' is indigenous to Sampson County, which encompasses Spivey's Corner, in the coastal plains of North Carolina. Aficionados of this "almost lost" art insist that it must not be confused with hog calling, nor with yodeling, which is done by mountain folks.

The easiest way to explain hollerin' to the uninitiated is that it is akin to Tarzan's call of the jungle, but far more complex. Hollerers modulate sound in their throats like Tarzan did, but also by changing the shape of the mouth cavity.

"For those who can't tell genuine hollerin' from screaming and yelling," Ermon Godwin and Oscar Bizzell helpfully tell us in *Hollerin' Revived at Spivey's Corner*, their history of the contest (through 1993), "there are four basic hollers that were practiced daily back before telephones came into being: the distress, the functional, the expressive, and the communicative."

The easily recognizable distress holler was a cry for help, "usually done in a falsetto tone and urgent sounding voice."

The functional holler, "often mislabeled as hog calling"— they really don't like that term!—is used to call in farm animals, but it also "let your neighbor know all is well, supper's on the table, or you need a fresh bucket of drinking water in the field."

The expressive holler is used in singing, "particularly if you don't know all the words of a song." It is considered "loud social conversation and is generally practiced just for the sheer ecstasy of hearing yourself."

All hollers are for the purpose of communication, but the communicative holler proper "is used simply to touch base with another soul. A man working alone in a field might holler just to hear a reassuring answer from his neighbor in the next field a mile or two away."

Naturally, as we enter the twenty-first century, hollerin' as a practical form of communication is long dead. That is the *raison d'être* of the hollerin' contest: to resuscitate and keep alive this traditional folk art. So now, hollerin', for the most part, takes place on the flatbed-trailer stage on the baseball field at Midway High School, on the practice field, or, as we shall see, in automobiles.

Out of the field of a dozen contestants in the thirty-second annual contest, there were actually two Yankees: John Harry, originally from Michigan, but now living in Shannon, North Carolina; and Steven "Corn" Alcorn, from Montville, New Jersey.

The Immortals of Hollerin' include past champions like Leonard Emmanuel, Floyd Lee, H. H. Oliver, and Henry Parsons. They have all gone home to Hollerin' Heaven now, but their talents (and those of six other former champs) are preserved for posterity on the Rounder CD, *Hollerin'*, recorded at Spivey's Corner in 1975 and 1976. They are also honored by contemporary contestants, who do their own renditions of the old-timers' hollers.

It was listening to, and falling in love with, this CD that brought "Corn" Alcorn to the stage to throw his voice into the mix. "We didn't have any cows or pigs to call," he told the predominantly Southern crowd, "but my buddies and I did have a holler up in New Jersey. If we were out play-ing and got separated, we'd holler 'eer-REET! eer-REET!' until we got back together."

Corn finished his set by hollerin' "You Are My Sunshine," in honor of former Louisiana governor (and author of the

tune) Jimmie Davis' birthday, followed by one chorus of
"How Great Thou Art" (the tunes of both, not the words). As
he left the stage to hearty applause, the emcee told him,
"That first one you did, Steve, we normally reach for a can
of WD-40 when we hear a sound like that."

You no doubt noticed that I tried to render Corn's holler
phonetically. His was relatively simple, but with the more
traditional hollers, I feel like the (Yankee) humorist H. Allen
Smith must have felt when he set out in the early 1950s to
write *The Rebel Yell*, in which he searches for the definitive
spelling of the titular yell. His research yielded nine candi-
dates—including "Woh-who-ey! who-ey! Woh-who-ey!
who-ey!" and "Errrrr-yahhhhhhhhhhhh-yip-yip-yip-yip-
yip!"—all of which were, to his mind—and mine, for that
matter—unsatisfactory. While I have rendered a few hollers
phonetically, as accurately as I could, my efforts are as unsatisfactory to me as Smith's were to him.

Only two old-timers competed this year. Eighty-seven-
year-old Lewis Foy Jackson of nearby Newton Grove con-
tributed a rousing, rapid-fire version of "that ol' rocking
chair song": "Well, takes a rockin' chair to rock/takes a
Cadillac to roll/takes a good looking woman just to satisfy
my soul/Keep on rocking/rocking all night long," but it
wasn't really hollerin' to my mind and I guess to the judges'

too, because he finished out of the money—or the glory, I should say, since a handsome trophy is the only prize.

"Hollerin' is communicating one with another, it's not about calling dogs or hogs or cows." That's the way Robey Morgan, eighty-five years old and two-time champion, opened his set. And he said it with a finality that brooked no disagreement, before doing versions of "Amazing Grace" and "Shortnin' Bread" that netted him a third place finish at the end of the day.

"I hope to do two things today," Larry Jackson, another two-time winner, told the crowd at the start of his set. "I hope to be able to entertain you and I hope to teach some of you something about hollerin'. One thing I'd like to teach you is an almost lost technique of hollerin', taught to me by my grandfather. It was real useful late in the afternoon, whenever you had a lot of echoes. It was hollerin' when you breathe out, and hollerin' when you breathe back in. This made the holler continuous and it carried a lot farther. See, when you got that technique down, then you could continue to holler right on and on, and you didn't have to stop and breathe, and the holler sounded a lot better.

"Another holler that was used was a 'good morning' holler. You had to let your neighbors know that you were up and about and everything was fine. You'd go out in the morning when you were feeding up your chickens, and you'd go: [untranscribable holler here]. And he'd hear that, and he'd know everything was fine over at your house, and he'd holler back, and you'd know everything was fine over at his house.

"Y'all have heard the term, all your life probably, whooping and hollerin'. Y'all know what hollerin' is, and I'd like to tell you what whooping is. Back a long time ago when they were going to send a message, they'd do a holler called a whoop. A whoop let your neighbors know, 'I'm fixing to send you a message.' This would distinguish this type of holler from one when they're hollerin' for just enjoyment. It went like this: HOOOOOO—OOOOOOH! HOOOOOO-OOOOOOH! If you wanted to let your neighbor know your hogs was out, you'd do a whoop holler and then a hog call: SUUUUUUUUUUU-EEEEEE! SUUUUUUUUUUUU-EEEEEEE! If he had seen your hogs, he'd holler back."

I told you it was complicated.

Larry ended his set with "Little Liza Jane," "Amazing Grace," and a distress holler so piercing that it brought the audience to its feet, each person ululating in their own personal style. It was quite impressive; I'll leave it at that.

Defending champion Tony Peacock, as expected, turned in a near flawless set, covering H. H. Oliver's version of the old chestnut, "Lulu My Darling," and closing out with an ear-splitting rendition of his signature good morning holler: LAA-OOOOOOO Lalalalalalalalalalalalalalala-LAH LAAA-O LAAA-O LAAA-O LAH WHOOOO!

If turnabout, as they say, is fair play, then it was fair enough that Kevin Jasper edged out Tony Peacock to take first place, just as Tony had done to him in 1999. Kevin had given an outstanding performance of expressive hollers, the high point being something called a "rolling waters holler," a special holler from the repertoire of one of the Immortals, Henry Parsons. I couldn't begin to put it down phonetically. The closest I can get is that it was kind of like drawn-out hiccups, a beautiful and awesome string of drawn-out hiccups.

Kevin Jasper was gracious in victory. "I live in Burlington, and work over in Wake Forest," he closed his acceptance speech. "It's about fifty miles back and forth. I got me a hollerin' tape, and I've spent hundreds of hours of listening to it. And I want to tell you, if ever you're on I-40 between Burlington and Wake Forest and you see somebody in an old Mercury Marquis doing this (he does a short burst of in and out hollerin'), you'll know it's either somebody having a coronary, or me practicing my hollerin'."

Part 2

WAY DOWN SOUTH

RARA in HAITI

Port-au-Prince, March 1994—There aren't many tourists in Haiti these days. Most every visitor here is a vampire of one sort or another, looking to suck something from the island nation: power, money, democracy, art, born-again Christian souls, drugs, adventure, a good deed well done, an understanding of why things have gone so wrong, vodou secrets, possibly a new life. I am no exception.

I came to rendezvous with Tina Girouard, a Cajun artist from Cecilia, Louisiana. She is completing a six-month residency to research a book on drapeaux vodou—voodoo flags—to which I will contribute the introductory essay. Tina had given me extremely precise instructions on how to negotiate the airport:

"You'll disembark the plane and walk across the tarmac. When you enter the terminal, go immediately to the immigration desks on your right and present your passport. When you're finished there, go out and to the left to the baggage area. There will be a gang of Haitians in brown uniforms with numbers on their chests hanging all over you to take your luggage, but just ignore them for the moment. Retrieve your own bags and then hand them over to one of the porters. They will carry them through the customs check and to the front of the terminal. Now this is where it gets tricky, so listen very carefully. Do not, I repeat, DO NOT go all the way to the street with your bags. As soon as you come through the front doors of the terminal, start looking for me. There are waiting areas for people meeting the flight on the right and on the left just outside the exit. I'll probably be the only *blanc* in the crowd, so just find me immediately and we'll hustle your bags to the car and go to the hotel."

It was a beautiful plan, beautifully executed on my part. It crumbled, however, as I strode out the exit, with a persistent taxi driver at my elbow, looked to my right and to my left, and found no one waving their arms at me in greeting.

I frantically scanned the reception areas a half-dozen times. Finally accepting this turn of events, I looked up to see my brown-capped porter and my bags exactly where they were not supposed to be—out in the street.

By the time I reached them, my bags were being fought over by nine or ten Haitian youths yelling at each other in

Kreyol. One of them, making himself heard above the fray, assured me in English, "I'm in charge, I'm in charge!" The porter, absolved of his duties, had his hand out.

Tina's plan had not included any information about Haitian currency or exchange rates, and a quick check of my pocket told me I was in trouble. The smallest U.S. bills I had were two fives, one of which I handed to the porter, who (most gratified) disappeared from my life.

I managed to stand my ground, searching the street and the crowd for some sign of Tina, for several excruciating minutes, until the taxi driver said, "M'sieur, maybe your friend does not come. This sometimes happens in Haiti."

I surrendered. I climbed into the ragged, late-model Chevy, and five or six of the more aggressive youths manhandled my three bags into the trunk. I offered up my last fiver, telling them to split it up among them (yeah, sure), and as the taxi pulled into traffic, the young fellow who had been "in charge" hung in the window demanding something for himself and letting me know, I'm positive, in Kreyol, just what kind of cheap, chiseling, back-stabbing, *blanc* bastard he thought I was.

I noticed my driver was not the man I had negotiated the fare with, but what the hell? He knew the way to the Hotel Oloffson, he spoke fair English, and he was attentive

and friendly in the way—I would discover during my trip—
that is typical of most Haitians.

He inquired if this was my first visit to Haiti (yes) and
presumed I must be a journalist (well, sort of, but I write
about art, not politics). Yes, he told me, he understood. But
this was a sad time for Haiti. With the embargo and all.
Gasoline was $30 a gallon. (Yes, I had read about that in *The
Miami Herald*.) Things were not like this before in Haiti, he
said, using a phrase I was to hear over and over while in
Port-au-Prince.

The drive up to this point had been unremarkable, but
as we turned onto Route Nationale 1, my introduction to
the suicidal nature of Haitian driving began. The cabbie
suddenly swerved to the left across the oncoming line of
traffic and screeched to a dusty halt. "Gasoline," he grinned
back at me, and then turned to speak rapidly in Kreyol to
a gaggle of people standing around a small wooden table
with three grimy one-gallon plastic containers atop it.

For some reason he did not share with me, his haggling
was unsuccessful. He started the Chevy and proceeded
along what, for brevity's sake, I'll call the shoulder of the
wrong side of the road, scattering pedestrians, attempting
now and again to break back across the oncoming traffic.

Unable to force any opposing driver to allow him through,

he did what had to be done. He wrenched the steering wheel to the right and floored it, causing a northbound Toyota to go sideways in a full slide, missing the Chevy by the barest. My driver fishtailed back into the southbound lane, leaving a cacophony of squealing brakes and curses in his wake.

About a mile down the road, he pulled over and cut the engine. Gesturing with one arm out the window, he grinned at me that he must speak with a girl and then loped across Route Nationale 1. Minutes later he returned. "Gas," he grinned at me. He retrieved an empty plastic container from the trunk of the cab and was off again.

I watched as several men helped him drain a gallon of gas from a fifty-five-gallon drum on the sidewalk across the way, as he borrowed a tin funnel, as he danced back to the car through traffic, poured the container into his tank, dodged back to return the funnel and spoke a few minutes again with his girl (she wore a smile and a bright blue dress), then returned to the cab with a shrug and a chuckle.

For the remainder of the trip, he drove with a furious recklessness I had not experienced since Da Nang in 1968. The pattern was this: gain as much speed as possible, turn off the ignition, free-cruise as long as possible, honking, passing on the right and on the left, making two lanes into three, plowing through crowds of pedestrians who avoided being run down with the grace of matadors, hitting the brakes only to slow down enough to twist the ignition key, pop the clutch, and jump-start the engine. Gain as much speed . . .

The only full stop after the gasoline purchase was at the gates of the Hotel Oloffson, where he had to shift into first gear for the steep climb up the driveway. I worried for the battered Chevy, but we made it, lurching and belching smoke, to the top. The engine was in its last flutterings when we stepped out of the taxi and heard the clang of the muffler falling onto the pavement. My driver was throwing it into the trunk as I climbed the hotel steps.

☾

"Carnival," the mulatto daughter of a well-to-do doctor told me, "was not like this before. The people come and drink and dance, true, but only because they must have some relief from the pressure we have been under for two years now."

It was the last night of Carnival, Fat Tuesday, my second night in Haiti, and I had been invited to join a party on the rooftop of the Clinique Rigaud, a one-story building on the parade route.

On my stroll down Rue Capois from the hotel, I encountered a familiar sight near the Champs de Mars, Port-au-Prince's Central Park. A group of men cracking whips had parted the crowd for a procession of Haitians masquerading as Indians in elaborate, sequined costumes. They were cousins of the Mardi Gras Indians of New Orleans, men who spend months creating grand suits of beads and sequins and feathers. The "Groupe Indien Du Xaragua," according to a hand-lettered sign carried by one member of the tribe, would have been right at home in the Crescent City chanting with the Wild Magnolias, the Yellow Pocahontas, the Golden Star Hunters.

Discounting one lone fellow in pink drag, the only other costumes in evidence that night were the police in their blue uniforms and the military in khaki. They were legion, with their Uzis and automatic pistols. They patrolled on foot through the crowded streets, and whole parades of them in brand new Jeeps—a line of twenty at one point—snaked along, pumping their weapons in the air in time to the music.

Carnival this year, I had been told, was a FRAPH celebration. An acronym for the Front for the Advancement and Progress of Haiti, FRAPH is a right-wing group of Duvalierists backed and given legitimacy by the military junta. They had a float of their own in the parade, with the only authentic vodou band at Carnival playing on it. As it passed the rooftop, a Reuters correspondent from Scotland pointed out "Toto" Constant, one of FRAPH's leaders, to me. Constant was sitting in the front. As I focused on him, he pulled a wad of money from his pants pocket, ostentatiously peeled off ten or twelve bills, and passed them back to the leader of the band.

I hate to admit it, but I thought the music on the FRAPH float was the best of the night. A fellow reveler on the rooftop of the Clinique Rigaud shared my view. The hypnotic vodou rhythms threw him to the ground, where he writhed uncontrollably; people rushed to him, covered his face with a towel, and tried to hold him still so he wouldn't hurt himself. It was the first time I witnessed a possession.

Leaving the festivities, I soon found myself caught in a logjam of human flesh. It was impossible to move more than a few inches in any direction. Tempers flared as a group of young men began to elbow their way through the crowd, who reacted in kind. A riot seemed imminent. It was scary.

Behind me, a policeman appeared and began knocking people this way and that. He began shoving me in the back. As if I could go anywhere. Great, I thought, the pressure drop right on me. The shoving turned into fisted blows. We were just below the FRAPH grandstand and I was the only *gwo blanc* (big white guy) in the vicinity and the gendarme probably wanted to show off for the big bad guys and for me it was the wrong place and the wrong time, but he didn't have enough room to wind up and really get his body into a punch and he hadn't landed a good shot to my kidneys that would have put me on the ground where I'd be tromped into a stupor or worse, and then somebody took his helmet and it disappeared forward on a sea of hands, because no one wanted to be caught holding the damn thing and have their brains beaten in or be shot dead, and his attention turned away from me and I bulled my way through the human logjam and briskly walked uphill to the Oloffson and lay on my bed in the four o'clock morning with a tall order of Rhum Barbancourt, listening to the boring one-note strains of the synthesizer-driven premier band of this "not like before" Carnival, Sweet Mickey, their name the same as the nickname of the strongman police chief of Port-au-Prince, Joseph Michel Francois.

☾

In most countries, at the end of Carnival, people go into the Lenten season of self-sacrifice, forgoing alcohol or chocolate or meat until Easter. Things are different in Haiti, where every season is one of sacrifice. In Haiti, Lent is a time for preparation for Rara, the vodouists' festival that begins a week before and then continues through Easter.

During the weeks leading up to the festival, Rara bands, usually headed by a houngan (a vodou priest), take to the streets for their "repetitions." Rhythms straight from Africa are played on drums, cylindrical tin scrapers, cowbells, bamboo horns called vaccins, anything percussive. There are chanting choruses of men and women, frenzied dancing and hearty consumption of clairin, a cheap and powerful raw rum moonshine with a sharply sweet aroma. The Rara bands are followed through the street of the poorest neighborhoods by hundreds, sometimes thousands, of dancing second-liners.

Tina, I learned on my arrival, had become marenn (godmother) to a Rara band in the Bel-Air section of Port-au-Prince, a dense mélange of decaying cinder block and corrugated tin dwellings sprawled over a hillside in the northern part of the city. She had been drawn there because of the concentration of flag makers—Tibout St. Louis, Joseph "Boss To" Fortine, Luc Cedor, Prospere Pierre-Louis, Yves Telemak, Clotaire Bazile, Edgard Jean Louis, Sylva Joseph. Tibout (Kreyol for "little bit"), though at eighty-two no longer making flags, was particularly helpful.

Born with only one arm, the other an elbow-length

stump, Tibout had the spirits in his head from an early age. His father was a houngan and by the time he was fifteen, Tibout had also become a vodou priest. His met tet (master of the head) is Legba, the crippled beggar at the crossroads, the intermediary between mortals and the pantheon of vodou loa (spirits), whose Catholic correspondent is St. Lazarus (not the one who was resurrected). Beginning in the 1930s, Tibout was for years the leader of a legendary Rara band, Autophonique. Because of his age, Tibout is now the mentor of his temple, the Société Lececoule Jour Mange, while his son-in-law, Luc Cedor, a priest and flag maker, manages the society.

It was as a tribute to Tibout and his history that Tina became godmother to this year's Rara. It is an honor, but one that includes certain responsibilities, primarily monetary: the women must have identical dresses, sequined vests must be sewn for the men, food and clairin must be purchased, the band must be paid.

I accompanied Tina and her guide and translator, Gesner Pierre, to Tibout's temple one afternoon to finalize plans for Rara. We parked on a one-lane street and entered the neighborhood, winding single-file down and around the mountain through narrow corridors not wider than three feet. Tibout greeted us in the peristyle of the thirty-foot-square temple, where several men were at small tables sewing sequins onto Rara chasubles. Luc Cedor joined us and we adjourned to the hounfor, the altar room.

The hounfor was small and dark (no electricity or running water in Bel-Air), so Luc lighted three candle stubs. On the altar was a four-foot cross, topped with a skull and surrounded by rum bottles and various talismans I could not make out. Listening to the singsong Kreyol of the two priests, the scene seemed completely natural.

It was decided that the Rara would be dedicated to Saint Isidore, who corresponds to the loa Papa Zaca (the farmer), and then we hiked to a meeting hall where Tina would be introduced to other members of the Rara group. It was to be a quick stop, but twenty people awaited us. Each of them made a short, animated speech. There was even a recording secretary, who read minutes of the ceremony.

Nightfall—not the best time to be out and about—was fast approaching as we followed Luc Cedor back through the winding corridors of Bel-Air, and in their gloomy darkness it was harder to avoid the streams of open sewage that trickled everywhere. Candlelight flickered from the one-room hovels as we passed, and the smell of food cooking over charcoal fires filled the air. We excused ourselves as we moved through small groups of people chatting on their "street corners." We were strange to them, but not strange, *blancs, blancs* with the houngan. Their soft, melodic *bon soirs* floated behind us as we passed.

🌙

The Hotel Oloffson has seen good days and bad, but at present it is again the place to be in Port-au-Prince. This is the place where "the truth is put into words every day, where rumor becomes history," according to the voiceover narrator of the docudrama *Traberg* by Danish filmmaker Jorgen Leth.

Leth (pronounced "Let"), who has permanent residency status in Haiti, is one of the usual suspects to be found at the bar or on the verandah of the Oloffson, which was built at the turn of the twentieth century as a private mansion. Leth is waiting for his Danish film crew to arrive to begin work on a documentary on vodou for the Discovery Channel. Meanwhile, he says he is "getting to know all the bad guys."

A *60 Minutes* crew is in town to do a piece on FRAPH. (Ed Bradley arrived the day I left.) Activist and pro-Aristide documentary filmmaker Rudy Stern, best known for *Haiti: Killing the Dream* (a censored version ran on PBS), is at the hotel with two assistants, being very secretive. Public health workers and embassy officials come and go. Child actor

Harley Cross arrives with his family from Jacmel on the coast
to swim in the pool. A short Colombian who speaks no
French or English checks in, has a hushed conversation with
two dark Haitian men, buys round after round at the bar,
checks out the next day. You notice these things.

Something always seems to be happening in Haiti, and
the Oloffson is where everyone comes to keep track of it.
The verandah receives a steady stream of reporters and pho-
tographers from the Associated Press, *The Miami Herald*, *The
Washington Post*, Reuters. They're here to feel everyone out
and withhold information.

There is no news in Haiti, only rumor. Word comes down,
for example, that General Raoul Cedras is having an afternoon press conference. Journalists scurry off. They return
only to say that the general was a no-show. Aristide will
name a new prime minister. But he doesn't. The junta will
name a new de facto government. But they don't.

☽

I had not been long in Haiti before I contracted Port-au-
Prince fever, an anxious torpor that settles on you unexpect-
edly. Your mind simply goes blank, as if your hard disk had
been erased. You begin to wonder, who am I? Where am I?
What am I doing here? The fever subsides. But not before

thoughts of the American Airlines flight that leaves each afternoon and how easy it would be to be on it drift through your head.

"For a visitor," Herbert Gold writes about Haiti in *Best Nightmare on Earth: A Life in Haiti*, "the country in 1963 was a laboratory in the business of manufacturing paranoia."

Thirty years later, business is still brisk.

The military show of force during Carnival was one example. Another was a scene that unfolded outside my hotel window one morning as I stood drinking coffee and looking at the garbage fires burning all over the city. I noticed there was a crowd of people staring up the street that runs to St. Gerard Church, whose priests and parishioners support Aristide and where antimilitary, pro-Aristide graffiti in bold red paint can still be seen.

As I craned to see the focus of their attention, I spied three men in civilian clothes throwing a young man to the ground. One of them held a pistol, which meant they were attachés, Macoute thugs paid and armed by the junta. They tied the captive's hands with rope and pulled him to his feet. A blow to the solar plexus put him back on the ground and a kick to the head sent him sprawling. Hauling him again to his feet, the gunman leveled his pistol at him and pulled the trigger. It didn't fire.

Maybe the gun was jammed. Maybe it was not loaded and the act was simply meant to terrorize the kid. Whatever, his captors got a good laugh out of it, and after punching him around some more, they threw him in the back of the car and drove off.

The crowd dispersed. The story was only of mild interest to the old Haiti hands at the Oloffson. Maybe he was a thief. Maybe he had the wrong political view. Either way, it had all happened so many times before. It would happen again. They were used to it, like they were used to the sporadic gunshots that rang out virtually every night I was in Haiti. Maybe "they" were only shooting in the air to keep everyone's nerves frayed. Maybe . . .

Port-au-Prince is the capital of the knowing look, the unfinished sentence, the all-encompassing Haitian shrug that is the final answer to most questions.

☽

Richard Morse, the current proprietor of the Oloffson, is a thirty-six-year-old Princeton graduate who stands six-and-a-half feet tall. He grew up in the States with his Haitian mother and his American father, a now retired dean of Latin American Studies at Yale. His first visit to Haiti was in 1975, and he relocated here in 1985.

When he took over the Oloffson, he reinstituted Monday night entertainment by a vodou dance troupe. He had played in a New York punk-rock band, the Groceries, during the early 1980s and had come back to Haiti to mine his musical roots—his mother, Emerante de Pradine, is a well-known musician and dancer, and his maternal grandfather, Eugene de Pradine, was a musician and composer who wrote the still popular Haitian folk ballad "Angelique," and was the arranger for the classic "Yellow Bird."

Morse married the lead dancer in the vodou dance troupe, with whom he has two children, and made her the centerpiece of a fifteen-member band he named RAM—for random access memory or Richard A. Morse, take your pick. RAM's music combines Morse's pop-rock tunes with authentic vodou rhythms, sung in Kreyol and English. It is an accessible, affecting, and hypnotic blend. (I witnessed my second possession during RAM's regular Thursday night gig.) Jonathan Demme, who travels often to Haiti and stays at the Oloffson, put RAM's "Ibo Lele" ("Dreams Come True") on the soundtrack of his movie *Philadelphia*.

Another regular at the hotel is Aubelin Jolicoeur. Make that the legendary Aubelin Jolicoeur, Petit Pierre from Graham Greene's *The Comedians* in the flesh. Small and dark, he is always impeccably dressed, usually in crispy starched and pressed white cotton, always carrying a silver tipped cane. Suave and flamboyant, he oozes intrigue. At one time, he liked to call himself the "son" of Papa Doc Duvalier. He was Minister of Tourism and Secretary of State for Information and Public Relations under Baby Doc. The "greatest journalist of Haiti," he writes for his own bi-weekly paper, *Le Nouvelliste*, as well as the daily *Le Matin*. He is, by his own admission, a man who possesses "both wit and wisdom." But it is dancing, he confided to a young woman at the bar one evening, that he considers his greatest success.

He and I had, in fact, been doing a bit of the Oloffson dance all week. I knew who he was, of course. Who in Haiti didn't? I also knew he knew who I was—there is little that escapes his attention. He had stopped to chat with someone I was at table with on two occasions, but had moved on with only the slightest acknowledgment of my presence. Another time, I was sitting with Tina and he came over to greet her, elaborately bowing and kissing her hand. Turning to me, he said, "Tina, you have told me everything about this gentleman, but you have not introduced him to me."

He insisted we join him, and my audience with Aubelin began.

Asking rhetorically if this was my first visit to Haiti, he explained to me that "things were not like this before," and launched immediately into a political discussion about the embargo, the total ineptitude of Aristide, and the arrogance of the American government—as opposed to me, personally—in trying to dictate to the Haitians, "who would have already solved this problem, if left to our own devices."

When I told him I found his frankness refreshing, that most Haitians I'd met had avoided talking about politics in such a way, he launched into a soliloquy that is indicative of the man when he is in full form.

"Ah, but Michael—I may call you Michael?—in Haiti politics is our life! What was it Aristotle said? Man is a political animal. And Aristide, his campaign for president was nothing but childish parables, kric krac stories for illiterate peasants. Is this an intelligent man? He is mad. He is a monster. It is time for people to understand this. I knew he could not stand.

"But the Haitians are a childish people. It has been said that the Haitian has the mind of a seven-year-old child. A Haitian would kill you for fun. It is true! He would shoot you just to see if his gun was working. Then he would hold his head and cry and moan. 'Oh, what have I done?'

"I have predicted these events that have taken place. People have called me a prophet. But I am not Cassandra! You remember what Apollo did to Cassandra? She could have the power to predict the future, but no one would believe her. I tell people—journalists from around the world—I am not Cassandra! Believe me! Believe what I say!

"But a prophet, Michael, as you know, has no standing in his own land. We have only to look at Jesus. Where was he first stoned? In Nazareth! Where he was born! They stoned him! He could have been killed! Telling the people that he was the son of God. He must be crazy! They knew him, you see. They knew he was the son of Mary and Joseph the carpenter. They knew this. Yes! He must be mad!"

☾

Even the routine has grand implications on the Oloffson verandah. The usual suspects become obsessed with Linda's story of the missing 60,000 condoms.

Linda—no last names, please, this activist requested—is based in Miami and works for a health organization. The mainstay of their efforts in Haiti is condoms, of which the organization had exactly none. She had expected to find an emergency shipment of 60,000 condoms waiting for her on her arrival in Port-au-Prince. They had disappeared.

Because their normal shipper had not completed the necessary paperwork to declare the condoms "humanitarian aid," her group had arranged to ship ten cartons of con-

doms to Haiti through the Seventh Day Adventists, who
have a huge compound outside Port-au-Prince, throwing
in five cartons of condoms for them for the favor. Now the
Adventist-in-charge could not be reached by telephone and
persistently would not return messages left for him. Linda
did not relish the irony of the situation—condom stealing
clerics?—as the rest of us did.

AIDS, of course, is a serious problem in Haiti. There are
no firm figures—estimates of those infected range from ten
percent to fifty percent—and AIDS prevention is one of the
goals of Linda's organization. But overpopulation is also
a serious threat to the stability of Haiti, and getting people
who are unaccustomed to using birth control to participate
in family planning is a difficult proposition. To leave those
involved in the program without their primary tool for
birth control, condoms, for over a month makes Linda's
blood boil.

On a Wednesday morning, two Haitians who work with
her group arrived at the Oloffson to drive Linda to a con-
frontation with the pastor. We drove south along the bay
toward the village of Carrefour. Lining both sides of the
road were the now familiar gasoline merchants with their
rows of plastic one-gallon containers. Every fourth vehicle
seemed to be a truck, a pickup, or larger, coming in from

the Dominican Republic loaded with drums of gas. There was a lot of it, according to our driver, and the price had come down to $20 a gallon. "Some say it will drop to $17 soon."

At the Adventist compound, there was no pastor. He was out in search of gasoline. Yes, he had been thus engaged for some time. Yes, the cordial Haitian woman could see that Linda had shipment papers for the condoms, but she knew nothing at all about it. Only the pastor would know about the shipment. Maybe they were still held at customs. Surely they could be picked up on Friday. It was a line of pure bullshit, delivered in the gracious Haitian manner, and the air-conditioning in the rather large office—gas-generated air-conditioning—flowed at full capacity during the entire exchange.

☽

The air was stifling in Tibout's temple and permeated with the odor of sweat and clairin. It was my last night in Haiti, and we had joined Luc Cedor and the Saint Isidore Rara group for a raucous dance through the streets of Bel-Air, at the end of which we snaked down the claustrophobic corridors to the temple, followed by hundreds of second-liners who crammed themselves into the peristyle.

I had been positioned on one of the concrete steps that make up a kind of bleacher up the south wall of the temple. The band continued to jam and chant, and Luc blasted on his whistle. He began to crack his bullwhip and clear a space around the center pole. A tall man performed a solo dance, twirling a baton, flailing this way and that, and breaking his fall by stabbing it into the dirt floor. He raised the baton in front of my face, lowered it over my head, and then rested it on my left shoulder as if he were knighting the *gwo blanc*, until Luc signaled the end of his solo with shrill whistling blasts and more cracking of his whip.

Two women in head scarves and long dresses stepped into the open space and began a fast shuffling dance, swaying from side to side with long swaths of fabric held in their outstretched hands. One of them undulated directly up to me. She took the fabric and gently swiped the sweat from my face and neck, and then fanned me for a few moments before backing rhythmically away.

Later at the hotel, I relished that Haitian gesture. But I also was haunted by a group of children, some as young as five, none older than ten, who had been having their own Rara repetition at Tibout's temple before the adults arrived. Their drums were plastic buckets, their vaccins were short lengths of PVC tubing, their scrapers were discarded pieces of tin bent into U-shapes and studded with nail holes, and the stand-in for a cowbell was a piece of iron struck with a rock. When the largest of them, the acting houngan, the boss, wanted to impose his idea of order on the group, he would pull a toy pistol from the back of his pants and brandish it at the others, yelling, until he got them arranged as he desired. When he stuck the gun back in his pants, he saw me watching and flashed a huge grin, as if we were sharing the biggest joke in the world.

Who knows, maybe we were.

OBSERVADOR por CASUALIDAD

EARLY SUNDAY MORNING 11 MARZO 2001. HOTEL MAJESTIC, ROOM 505. I am standing at the front window of my fifth-floor suite, taking in the majestic view of the Zocalo—the Cathedral en diagonal to my left; across the way, the Palacio Nacional; to my right, the Regencia De La Ciudad; and beyond it across Pino Suarez, the Suprema Corte De Justicia. It is a beautiful, bright sunshiny day, and the crowd below is a mere fraction of what it will be when Subcomandante Marcos and the ZapaTour arrive in a few hours.

Miguelo, I say to myself, you are one lucky son of a bitch.

If not for an improbable string of lucky accidents, you see, I would not be in Mexico City at all. I would be sitting at my computer at home in New Orleans, reading about this historic day in the online version of *The New York Times*.

Novelista Barry Gifford, mi amigo viejo, invited me to accompany him to the XVII Festival Del Centro Histórico

De La Ciudad De México from 7 Marzo to 11 Marzo. It was a free trip, except that nothing is ever free: we both had to fly from the same airport, which meant I had to pay my own way to California. Por casualidad, by accident, I had a free round-trip plane ticket earned from frequent-flyer miles that I could use to fly to Oakland, where I joined Barry and the Mexican author Juvenal Acosta and we continued on to Mexico City.

Originally, the Festival had booked "Barry Gifford and guest" into the Holiday Inn, but Barry told them that was unacceptable, and por casualidad we ended up at the Majestic.

Our scheduled flight back to the U.S. left early on 11 Marzo, but when I learned that was the day the ZapaTour—Marcos and his Zapatista followers—was arriving from Chiapas after many days on the road, I extended my stay. Barry left that Sunday morning, and I moved from my small "guest" room into Barry's "Star" suite—the beautiful, the spacious Room 505, overlooking the Zocalo. My observation post.

Casualidad? Fortuna? Destino? Take your pick.

SNAPSHOTS FROM THE DAYS
LEADING UP TO 11 MARZO

SNAP: WEDNESDAY. Guillermo Arriaga, who wrote the screenplays for *21 Grams* and *Amores Perros*, which was nominated for an Oscar for Best Foreign Film in 2001 (alas, it did not win), and Mauricio Montiel, of *Cambio*, Gabriel Garcia Marquez's new, soon-to-be-launched weekly magazine, take Barry, Juvenal, and me to the Mercado Sonora. Because of the book and movie, *Perdita Durango*, people think Barry has an interest in *santeria*, when in reality he is ambivalent about it. I, on the other hand, buy a beautiful black and red necklace, made from some kind of small seeds, to honor Elegua (known as Legba in Haiti) for all the doors he has opened for me on this trip.

SNAP: THURSDAY. A luncheon at the residence of the U.S. Embassy's Cultural Attaché, al fresco. A garden party. The arrival of the ZapaTour on Sunday is mentioned. An African-American *señora* says, "Oh my, I was hoping to do some shopping on Sunday."

SNAP: FRIDAY. I see the flamboyant performance artist Astrid Hadad at La Bodega in the La Condesa neighborhood. She comes onstage wearing a wedding dress and a black ski mask and sings a satirical song about Subcomandante Marcos. "I know you are a genius," I tell her after the show, "and if I understood more Spanish, I'd know why." She tells me, "It will take a few years before anyone can say anything real about Marcos."

SNAP: SATURDAY. Being a turista on Correo Mayor. A boom box is blaring Elvis' "Jailhouse Rock." I think of the Zapatistas still in prison. I don't think they are rocking.

SNAP: SATURDAY NIGHT. Mayra Gonzalez and her friend Carlos take me to the oldest cantina in Mexico City, El Nivel (The Level), just steps off the Zocalo down Cinco de Mayo. No sign, only two screened doors covered with aluminum, so you can't see in. To keep out unwanted turistas. A local joint and they want to keep it that way and I don't blame them. A mechanical device on the wall measures how much the city is sinking, how level it is. Above this device, there is a painting of Subcomandante Marcos embracing a nude

woman. I ask, "Why is he embracing the Naked Maja?" No
one knows the answer. Or no one is telling.

SNAP: LATER SATURDAY NIGHT. Carlos is driving
through the San Angel barrio. From the back seat I say,
"This place looks so familiar. The buildings, these narrow
streets, that little hill over there. I've seen all this before. I
had a dream about riding in a car in this neighborhood."
Mayra asks, "You had this dream last night?" and I tell her
no, no, it was some time ago. She asks if this happens to
me often. I tell her, yes, it does actually. Déjà vu, she says,
but I say it is more like precognition, seeing something
before it happens. She asks, "Were you kidnapped in the
dream?" "No," I tell her. "That will be the difference here,"
Mayra says, laughing.

SNAP: EVEN LATER SATURDAY NIGHT. We are at Bar
La India in El Centro Histórico. Carlos and Mayra are drinking cerveza, and I am eating sopa azteca. Answering my
question, Carlos says, "It is a complicated situation. I support the cause of the *indígenas*. But Marcos? He is a myth, he
is all smoke." Mayra says, "Whatever you write, I want to

be on the side of the Indians." I tell her, "Of course you do, you *are* on their side. We're *all* on their side! Look, what I know about Marcos and the EZLN would not fill a glass of beer, but I do know *los Indios* are getting screwed. A monkey knows that! *Los Indios* always get screwed. It doesn't matter what country it is, if there are *Indios*, they are getting screwed." On the TV hanging from the ceiling in the back corner of the cantina, Marcos is being interviewed. He is puffing out a tremendous cloud of smoke from his pipe. So much smoke it seems affected, theatrical, lame. What does that mean? Does it mean anything?

SUNDAY AFTERNOON 11 MARZO. I had no plan of action when I went over to the Zocalo. I just wanted "to be among *mi gente*," as I phrased it later to Juvenal when he telephoned to see how the day was going. "How were 'your people'?" he asked, laughing. What I tell you now is basically what I told Juvenal—*pero con mas detalles,* but with more details.

All the streets leading to the Zocalo were blocked off, with policemen checking purses and backpacks for weapons or bombs. As I cleared the checkpoint at the end of Madero Street, I noticed what seemed to be green paper money lying here and there. I picked up one of the bills and found that it was a *"20 Pueblos"* bill issued by *El Barzon de Nuevo León Padre Mier* in the name of *"Pueblo De México."* The bill listed the telephone number, website, and email address for the organization. Several slogans were printed on the bill also: *"No Lo Tires, Daselos A Quier Mas Quieras," "Esta Lana Es De Colección," "Reconocimiento De Los Derechos y Cultura Indígena."* I put the bill in my pocket. You never know.

In the middle of the street—I never understood whether it was M. de Piedad or 5 de Febrero on this block—a large audience had formed around two bare-chested young men beating out Afro-Cuban rhythms on hand-drums. Inside the open space with the drummers, two boys and a girl, each in their own world, were dancing with wild abandon, as the crowd cheered them on. A costumed man on stilts walked by. Who he was supposed to be and where he was going, or why, I could not tell you. A clown dressed in a suit of bright colors, with a red ball nose and big floppy shoes, strolled back and forth, back and forth. He was not doing anything particularly funny, just flirting with every woman who passed by. As we say in New Orleans, "Ain't nothing but a party going on!"

On the perimeter of the Zocalo, the atmosphere was

much like a rock concert. There were scores of vendors selling t-shirts, t-shirts, and more t-shirts, bearing various
EZLN slogans and images of Subcomandante Marcos. One
woman was even selling Manu Chao t-shirts!

My favorite image was on a white t-shirt: a black skele-
tal hand—palm out as if to say "Alto!"—printed over a red
star, with a bold black "EZLN" beneath it on the front. On
the back, all in black letters, is the handprint again and
twisting around it the words: "Coge El Fusil y Baila," Grab
a Gun and Dance. (I am wearing one as I write this.)

There were Subcomandante Marcos bandanas, baseball
caps, and ski masks. There were so many vendors scattered
all over selling so many things that for all I know there
were Subcomandante Marcos pipes, watches, beer mugs,
underwear, and jigsaw puzzles for the kids.

Wherever there is a huge crowd of people, no matter in
what country they are gathered, no matter the event—a
wrestling match, a visit by the Pope—these gypsy vendors,
these intrepid entrepreneurs, will be there. Without fail. With
anything and everything they think a person might buy in
the heat of the moment. They are legion. They will have their
blankets spread on the ground outside the Gates of Hell.

Once I was in the crowd, it did not seem as daunting as it had from the window of 505. I decided to cut across to 20 de Noviembre, the street the ZapaTour would be taking to enter the Zocalo. By the time I got to the chain link fence that had been erected to keep people from storming the caravan, however, I had missed the bus with Subcomandante Marcos. I do not deal well with disappointment, so this situation was totally unsatisfactory. I became determined to see Marcos with my own eyes.

A large, covered stage had been erected on the Cathedral side of the Zocalo for a "Welcome Zapatistas" rock concert headlined by the popular local band *Maldita Vecindad* on Monday, tomorrow. It had a state-of-the-art sound system, and beside it was a gigantic television screen for broadcasting the concert, or anything for that matter—something like an historic political rally. But for some reason that escaped me, the Zapatistas were to speak from a small uncovered platform, with one microphone on a stand, set up on the east side of the Zocalo, with the Palacio Nacional in the background.

In any large, dense crowd, there are always rivulets of movement, so I surveyed the Zocalo to see how I could best get to the ZapaTour stage. There were two raised platforms for television camera crews set at angles to either end of the stage, with a considerable open space between them. To get to that opening and a straight-on view of the stage, I needed to move to my left. I eased into the closest flowing stream of people, planning to change course into tributaries as necessary to gain access to my objective. I was unable to make this maneuver, however, finding myself being carried inescapably to my right.

I am flexible. I made a new plan. I would stay with the rivulet I was trapped in and get around the camera platform at the south end of the stage, from which position I would have a fair sight line to Marcos. This Plan B was a good plan, but it too met with failure. I found myself directly behind the camera platform, with a perfect view of the asses of the crew members.

Mi compadres were as frustrated as I was, but much less restrained. Many of them began to angrily shout at the TV people and give them the finger. There was a steady chanting of *"Bagense! Bagense!"* There were cries of "Fuck the press!" and "Motherfuckers!" At one point, some in the crowd began to throw things at the camera crews: wadded paper cups, plastic bottles, and (thank God!) other non-lethal missiles.

At this point, I noticed that people were crawling under the platform, contorting themselves through the aluminum supports. It was considerably more difficult for me than for the shorter Mexicans, and I certainly did not make any new friends, but I was able to make the trip myself. The good news was that I was about sixty feet from the stage. The bad news was that I was only seven feet in front of the camera platform and I was not going anywhere else, forward or backward.

Did I mention how fucking hot it was in the Zocalo?

So there I stand—pouring sweat, wedged in so tight that it is impossible for me to get a cigarette from my pocket and light it—a gringo whose most used Spanish phrase is "Hable mas despacio, por favor." (Please speak more slowly.) And there are speakers before Marcos. And Marcos is introduced, but then he introduces a few other speakers. And then Marcos begins his speech. A chant rings out: "Marcos, Duro! Marcos, Duro! Marcos, Duro! Bravo! Bravo!" And another, fuller and louder: "EL PUEBLO UNIDO JAMÁS SERÁ VENCIDO!! EL PUEBLO UNIDO JAMÁS SERÁ VENCIDO!!" (The People United Will Never Be Defeated!!)

And in this historic moment, *very in* this historic moment, Marcos speaks holding a thick stack of pages in his hand—and all I can think is, Please God, let the type on those pages be *muy grande!*

MIDNIGHT AT THE MAJESTIC 11/12 MARZO. The only light burning in 505 was the bedside lamp I was using to read myself to sleep. I was almost there, when I heard the sound of drums coming from the Zocalo. As the drumming continued in a steady rhythm, I got up and walked to the front window. Leaning on the windowsill, I saw a group of maybe 100 people gathered over toward the Regencia De La Ciudad. I could see a small campfire starting to blaze, and in front of it two drummers wearing only headbands, loincloths, and knee-high moccasins. I had seen Indian dance troupes performing in the Zocalo on Saturday, but why would they be performing at this hour? If it wasn't a dance troupe, what the hell was going on?

Now wide awake, I got dressed quickly and walked over to the Zocalo. The group was indeed *Indios.* They had formed into three concentric circles, and they were obviously performing some sort of ritual or ceremony. There was an inner circle around the fire and the drummers that consisted of the elder who was conducting the ceremony and his acolytes—where the magic was being done, I thought. About twenty paces out from the inner circle, members of the group formed another circle, and twenty paces out from them another larger circle was formed. There was much chanting and dancing, and much burning of copal incense. At intervals, the two outer circles would conjoin with the inner circle, the elder would murmur an incantation too low for me to hear, and the three circles would form again.

Suddenly a very bright light exploded behind me, and when I turned toward it, I saw a three-person TV crew interviewing a Mexican gentleman. The interview was over in less than five minutes, and I approached the interviewee, thinking: this is the man who can tell me what is going on here. Well, sort of. He spoke less *inglés* than I spoke *espagnol*, but I did manage to learn that I was witnessing a New Year's ceremony, that today, 12 Marzo, was a new day, a new month, a new year.

At midnight, there had been maybe two dozen spectators, but by 2 a.m. there were only a half-dozen. One fellow who had been there since the beginning of the ceremony was a striking figure. He was wearing a dark overcoat, with his pants legs tucked into combat boots. His hair was cut short, he wore round wire-rim glasses, and he had a small goatee that swept upward from his chin into a point. In short, he looked like Leon Trotsky. I decided two things: he knows what is going on, and he speaks *inglés*. And he did, and he did.

His name was Miguel Angel Rogers—a Mexican whose grandfather was Irish—and he gave me a printed announcement that explained the gathering: El calpulli Nexticpac de Anáhuac 2000 A.C. tiene el honor de invitarie a la celebración del año 5722 de nuestra cuenta propria, que corresponde al ano nahua Ome Calli "dos casa." I was witnessing an Anáhuac Indian ceremony for the New Year 5722.

Another happy accident! It was too much. After spending the day with thousands of people who were packed into the Zocalo to support los derechos y cultura indígena (the rights and culture of indigenous Mexicans)—and to buy t-shirts—I had the rare privilege to be present at a ceremony performed by descendents of *indígena* who walked this ground almost 6,000 years ago. And there was hardly anybody there!

Santa Maria! It slipped my mind: Toward the end, I had been aimlessly looking around the area, and standing in the glow of the street lights at the edge of the Zocalo at 16 de Septiembre, I saw the ugliest transvestite I have ever seen in my life—and I have lived in New Orleans for twenty years, which means I have seen a lot of transvestites. This one had a long pockmarked face, and seeing it was like a hard slap to the head. She was wearing a nice low-cut blue-sequined dress and large silver pumps that did not go well

with it. You know how dwarfs' bodies are oddly propor-
tioned? Her body was like that, except she was tall. She
stood shyly and quizzically watching the ceremony, and I
felt a deep sadness for her. Her life could not be an easy one.

I turned my attention to the Anáhuacs for a moment,
then shifted my gaze back toward the transvestite—all writers are voyeurs and eavesdroppers—but she was not there.
It was eerie. Eerier than her appearance. There was too much
open space in every direction for her to have disappeared
so quickly. No way. But, she had.

What did that mean? Did it mean anything?

The ceremony was elaborate and moving, and I was moved.
Acolytes carrying pottery censers full of glowing copal
went around both outer circles, stopping at each person
and bathing them from toe to head, front and back, with
the smoke of the copal, cleansing them for the new year.
In procession, the elder and his acolytes walked around
the second circle and made offerings to the cardinal points
of the world. They went first to the East, then South, West,
North, and back at the campfire there were offerings to the
Heavens. Thanks for a new year were offered up by various
Anáhuacs, and continually, obeisance was paid to Ome-

teotl, God of Duality—Life and Death, Good and Evil, and so on.

Ometeotl, Miguel Angel explained, was the god who resided in the thirteenth heaven with Ometecuhtli, called "Two Lord," who held a drop of water in his hands and in this drop of water was a green seed, which was the earth surrounded by the ocean. Or the two gods were part of each other—I got a little confused.

Two acolytes, a woman holding a goblet and a man with a large pottery bowl, stood in front of the Anáhuac to my left. The bowl carrier poured some liquid into the goblet, and the acolytes moved around the circle, emptying and refilling the goblet, until each person in the circle had drunk from it. The last person served was just to my right. I noticed for the first time that the woman acolyte looked exactly like my psychiatrist—Dr. Janet Johnson—at the Veterans Hospital in New Orleans, where I go to have my grasp of reality monitored. While pondering this, she surprised me by stepping outside the circle, offering me the goblet, and gesturing for me to drink—which I did. What else? When I tried to give it back to her, she smiled and gestured that I should move the goblet in a circle with both hands and drink again, which I did. I was told later that the goblet contained ceremonial *pulque*. It was the first drink of alcohol I had had in three years.

When the ceremony concluded, it was four in the morning. The Anáhuacs gathered around the fire and began to remove parcels from cloth bags and backpacks. We could not make out what was going on, so Miguel Angel walked over for a closer look. When he returned, there was a big smile on his face, and his eyes were twinkling like a child's on Christmas morning.

"They have brought food," he said. "They are having potluck!"

THREE FAREWELLS

The "CITY LIGHTS BOOKSTORE" of BIRMINGHAM, ALABAMA

PROP. GENE CRUTCHER:
A Rememberance

I met Gene Crutcher sometime in 1962, the year he opened his bookstore in Birmingham's Southside neighborhood known as Five Points, because five streets and avenues converged on a traffic circle. I was a fifteen-year-old Woodlawn High School student that year, and my buttoned-down suburban life had just been seriously altered by reading *The Dharma Bums* by Jack Kerouac. Discovering Gene Crutcher—Books finished off the job.

The bookstore became, literally, a substitute for school. Many was the day I skipped classes, hitchhiked to Southside, and spent the day reading and bullshitting with Gene.

It was around this time that I made the decision that I was going to be a writer. My ambition was encouraged and

supported by Gene and his wife Bettie, who was the greatest. In the life I was leaving behind, being a writer was just
not a thought anyone would have, but at Gene Crutcher—
Books, the aspiration was not only taken seriously, it was
considered completely *normal*.

I have thought about it, but I cannot remember any specific books Gene recommended to me during those early
years of my writing life. I didn't look to him as a guru, but
I respected his reading suggestions, which overall simply
pointed me along the direction I was already heading on
my own. In any case, Crutcher's reading was eclectic and
eccentric. Often it was cursory; he knew about, and could
talk about, books which he had never read and had no real
interest in, other than to keep up his end of a conversation.
He was a great bullshitter. He had a great love of poetry,
though at times I found him less than discerning; he loved
the reading of it and the reading of it aloud. (He was blessed
with a fine, deep reading voice.) He had a passion for sci-
ence fiction, which I could never share with him. In my
memory, Farley Mowat was his favorite author, and to this
day I have never read one of his books.

While Gene was old enough to have had a son my age,
I did not consider him a father figure, anymore than I did
a guru. Like many adolescent boys, especially those read-

ing Beat writers and Zen Buddhist scriptures (in Bible Belt Alabama!) and writing poetry, I was not getting along with my own father and certainly had no need for another or a substitute. And while over the ensuing years I came to feel like a member of the Crutcher family, Gene was essentially a friend. A damn good one.

I went to college at the University of Alabama, sixty miles west of Birmingham in the small town of Tuscaloosa, from 1964 to 1966, and the many weekends I was back in Birmingham always included at least one visit to the bookstore, to catch up on things. From 1966 to 1968, I was in the Marine Corps and had my first wife send me books from Crutcher's, keeping in touch that way. When I returned from Vietnam in the fall of 1968 and enrolled at the University of Alabama-Birmingham, Gene offered me a job and I took it. I was his assistant for two years, and it was a wild, crazy ride. Everything that was "happening" in town was either dreamed up at Crutcher's or announced first from there. It wasn't a job, it was a calling.

It was during this period that I became inextricably caught up in the lives of the Crutcher family. Bettie was always around, ostensibly the bookkeeper (until that became a moot point), when she wasn't busy with their kids: Annie, Beth, Kay, twins Bill and David, and Sara. And the kids, in varying combinations, were constantly in and out. Throw in the steady stream of wackos coming through the store and we were one big extended family. Somewhat dysfunctional, to be sure, but a family nonetheless.

It's not easy being married, period, and it wasn't easy being married to Gene Crutcher. He had a lecherous streak that was hard for him to control. He loved photography and probably had a photo of *every single* customer who ever came into the store, as well as a considerable collection of females baring their breasts for the camera. He was hopelessly impractical, especially when it came to money, of which there was never enough. He could be cantankerous and pigheaded and inconsiderate. Consequently, he and Bettie had some furious rows, both at home and in the bookstore, damn whoever was around. But it is easy to assess the shallows of love; the depths are far murkier.

I left town for a year or so, and when I returned late in 1971, Gene gave me my old "job" back. Things were bad financially and got progressively worse. I stayed on with him until close to the end of the bookstore era, when nobody could pretend any longer that things would get turned around. It was an insane situation. I did it because I felt it was the thing to do, and because I loved the guy. I had an hourly salary for awhile, then it came to Gene squeezing out enough money for me to pay my rent and buy groceries, and after that a few bucks here and there for a cheap date or a few beers with the guys. I filled in with freelance writing and an odd job now and again.

One afternoon toward the end, one of my creditors (unpaid and unremembered now) called to talk to Gene about garnishing my salary. "Salary," Gene thundered in his profoundest *basso*, "salary! He doesn't have a salary. We're sinking here like an anvil in the sea!" Whereupon, creditor folded into the mists of time, and Gene and I quaffed several of his infamous homebrewed beers (poured carefully into glasses, with care not to stir up the foul sediment at the bottom of the bottle) and laughed our asses off, over and over throughout the afternoon.

By the end of 1973, Bettie had been undergoing dialysis treatment (which she hated) for some time and the kids were getting older, all in school and all that, and his personal financial needs outstripped his earnings. Literally, he had to rob Peter to pay Paul: Peter being publishers and book and magazine distributors, and Paul being everybody who could foreclose on his immediate personal life. It didn't work. It couldn't and it didn't and in 1974 Gene Crutcher—Books was over.

It's all in memory now. Like the visit by Allen Ginsberg,

who put Crutcher at the center of joy in the universe by pro-
claiming that his bookstore was the City Lights Bookstore
of Birmingham and drawing his fish graffiti and word bless-
ing on the bathroom wall—the same visit that long-gone Joe
Simpson wrote a poem about that was published in *The Ever-
green Review* and cost him his position as a judge in Mountain
Brook, the richest suburb of Birmingham and one of the richest in the nation. Like the afternoon I was sitting at the front
desk and Chuck Berry came into the store looking for a copy
of "Casey at the Bat," which (surprise!) we didn't have, and
when I excitedly told Gene that Chuck Berry (!) was in the
store, he said, "Who the hell is Chuck Berry?" Like a thousand, at least, lesser but no less important stories that could
be told. All in memory. As Bettie is. As Gene is.

I tell people that Gene Crutcher—Books was where a lot
of people went to fuck up their lives. And it's true. And I
mean that in the most positive way. The books I bought
there, the books I read there without paying for, the dis-
cussions and arguments (sane and insane) I had there, the
good and true and close friends I made there and who
remain so four decades later—I wouldn't trade it for anything. (And I couldn't if I wanted to; so be it.)

Whatever Birmingham is in 2004, during the 1960s it was
a close-minded, religiously fundamentalist, racist back-

water town. Gene Crutcher—Books was a place where people who were not proud of those attributes could go and commune together and connect to a larger, better world. Racial equality, philosophy, politics, poetry and literature, art and music were the topics *du jour*. It was a *compliment* when the Ku Klux Klan burned a cross on the roof. There was simply no place like it. It was an institution, goddammit, and the inmates ran it. The regulars included beatniks and later hippies, communists, civil rights workers and supporters, judges, college professors, students, nudists, the hip and the square, crackpots of every stripe, artists, musicians, and, always, writers. It was the nerve center of a "community" in search of itself.

Gene opened the bookstore, naturally enough, to make a living at something he enjoyed, and it must have bemused him, in his quietest moments, that he became the facilitator for a cultural revolution in Birmingham that mirrored the one going on in the rest of the nation. He also loved it. He had enough of the ham in him (more than enough, some would say) to relish his place on the stage. And for all his faults, he was gracious enough to allow his fellow players room to develop their own parts.

Having lived in New Orleans for fifteen years, I had not, to my great chagrin now, had any contact with Gene for a long spell, but on a Sunday night—October 26, 1997—as I was driving in a torrential downpour between the towns of Panacea and Apalachicola in the Florida panhandle, out of nowhere, he came into my thoughts: Man, I haven't seen or talked with Crutcher in a long time. Wonder what he's up to? He's not getting any younger. He's not going to live forever. I gotta give him a call.

The next night, I got a call from Birmingham, an old friend telling me that Gene had died the night before.

Goddamn! It was like his spirit, on its way to wherever, had passed by to tell me, in a voice I couldn't make out in the lightning and thunder, "Too late, mullethead."

MY FRIEND WILLIE MORRIS, 1934–1999, in 900 WORDS

A little after eight o'clock on the morning of August 3, 1999, my wife shook me out of a deep sleep. "I've got bad news," she said, handing me a folded section of the newspaper. The headline was large enough for me to read without my glasses: "Southern voice is silenced." My friend Willie Morris, the noted Mississippi editor and writer, had died of cardiomyopathy at 6:21 p.m. the night before. He was only sixty-four years old.

The only other time Willie had caused me to be awake at that time of the morning—he was a notorious night owl and late sleeper—was back in 1995. My wife handed me the phone that morning too, and there was Willie. He was in New Orleans to promote his new book *My Dog Skip*, and had apparently been up all night. "I'm going over to the Acme and have a dozen oysters on the half shell, while you wake up," he said, in that slow, precise way he had when he was up to something, and like Tom Sawyer, he was always up to something. "And a Bloody Mary, that sounds nice. Maybe two. Meet me at Galatoire's at eleven for lunch."

He arrived at the restaurant as excited as a kid on Christmas morning. "I just purchased 280 dollars worth of figurines (he pronounced it "figgereens") at the toy soldier shop on Royal Street," he told me, "so whatever you do, don't let me forget to pick them up."

There was some sort of military medal pinned askew to his lapel, and when I inquired about its significance, he said, "I was compelled to give myself a Good Conduct Medal." That was Willie.

A lot of stories about Willie take place in the wee hours and revolve around drinking, because he was undeniably a man who liked a drop. As his friend Orley Hood, a senior editor at *The Clarion-Ledger* in Jackson, Mississippi, so aptly puts it, "He was good for the soul, and bad for the body."

Willie also liked to talk, just for the sheer pleasure of it, and he could talk about anything for hours on end, though his favorite topics were writing, writers, and baseball. He possessed an "encyclopedic knowledge," in the words of novelist William Styron, "and an elegantly furnished mind."

Dr. Johnson once said about one of his acquaintances that he was not only dull, he induced dullness in others. Willie was just the opposite. He was so smart and witty and full of life and hijinks that he infected everyone who was in the room with him and lifted them to his level.

Willie burst onto the national stage in 1967, when he became the eighth editor of *Harper's Magazine* in its (then) 117-year history, and at thirty-two, the youngest to ever hold that position. In short order, he turned that venerable but stodgy publication into possibly the best magazine this country has ever seen, certainly the one most involved in the major events of its times of any magazine before or since. A list of the writers he published reads like a who's who in American letters. Among their number were C. Vann Woodward, David Halberstam, Larry L. King, Marshall Frady, John Updike, Truman Capote, Arthur Miller, and Norman Mailer.

But after only four heady years, Willie was forced to resign, for being, well, too Willie. "It all boiled down," he said at the time, "to the money men and the literary men. And as always, the money men won." In short order, his contributing editors also resigned.

It was also in 1967 that Willie published his first book, *North toward Home*, a memoir about the intellectual and emotional exodus he had been forced into by the intransigent racism of the deep South in general and his home state of Mississippi in particular. The book became a beacon of light for expatriate Southerners everywhere. That would be a recurring theme in more than a dozen other books he published in the last half of his life, a delving into his own history and the history of the South in an effort to explain both not only to the nation and the world, but to Southerners themselves and to himself: *Yazoo: Integration in a Deep Southern Town* (1971), *Good Old Boy: A Delta Boyhood* (1971), the woefully under-appreciated *The Courting of Marcus Dupree* (1983), *Faulkner's Mississippi* (1990), *New York Days* (1993), and *The Ghosts of Medgar Evers* (1998).

Willie will be remembered by posterity for the great writing he has left us, but his many friends will remember his unbounded generosity, his steadfast loyalty, and the unequaled pleasure of his company, especially the hilarity of his practical jokes, which were a constant in his life. Like the time he called David Duke's campaign headquarters on the night of the 1992 Louisiana gubernatorial elections and asked to speak to Eva Braun. He was asked to hold on, and over the open line he could hear Eva being paged.

Someone came back on the line, told Willie that Eva didn't answer the page, and asked him to describe her. "She's blonde," Willie told him, "very Germanic looking."

It could easily have been Willie who set down the line

penned by his fellow Mississippian McKinley Morganfield, a.k.a. Muddy Waters: "There's a whole lotta things I ain't never done, but I ain't never had too much fun."

That would have been a fitting epitaph for my pal Willie.

SAD in my HEART

(for GEORGE HARRISON)
November 30, 2001 — Mexico City

I woke up this morning in my small apartment in Calle de Mesones just off Isabel La Catolica, and as I usually do first thing, I reached over and clicked my boombox from CD mode to FM radio. 88.1 FM radio "RED," a station broadcasting under the auspices of one of the many universities in Mexico City, I know not which. Nor do I know what the "RED" means, though it is always emphatically pronounced. I found it by accident one day and have stuck with it, because it has lots of cultural interviews and news and commentary that I try to understand and improve my Spanish. "Habla mas despacio, por favor" I say over and over to the announcers, "please speak more slowly," but they never do. On the brighter side, when they are not speaking *mas rápido*, they play a wonderfully interesting mix of music in Spanish and *inglés*.

On this morning I am writing about, a George Harrison song was playing. Then another. Brushing away the last cobwebs of sleep, I knew he had gone on home, as the saying goes. And then the 88.1 FM "RED" announcer confirmed it for me, *despacio* this time.

George, oh George, not my "favorite Beatle" by any means, but I wanted to hear somebody doing "Another Man's Done Gone" in his honor—preferably Sugar Blue blowing harmonica on his instrumental version of that moving funereal blues, but it was only playing in my head.

I had not been reading newspapers, Spanish or English language, for weeks, because I had come to Mexico City in large part to distance myself from the shameless uses another George, G. W. Bush, and his cronies were making of the September 11 Al Qaeda attacks on the World Trade Center in New York City—"the day that changed everything in America"—doing their best to turn tragedy and the "war to eliminate evil" into more shovelsful of money for the insatiable fat cats who want paradise now, goddammit, and plenty of it. The only television I saw was *fútbol* in the cantinas.

My point here being, I did not know that George Harri-

son had any kind of cancer countdown until hearing it one
afternoon some days back, from my friend Christofer, the
beer-drinking-only Dean Moriarity of Chihuahua, México,
at Beto's Cantina on Calle Dolores, while eating a delicious
sopa de pasta. (Christofer is a high-school history teacher, or
so he says, and a raconteur of the highest order, who loves
his cerveza and has never met a man who was not his friend.
He is laying low at a cheap hotel in my neighborhood,
because of some kind of trouble back home in Chihuahua,
trouble that has to do, as far as I can ascertain from his
sketchy details, with a woman who is not his wife, possibly his secretary.)

   I listened to a few more Harrison tunes as I dressed, and
pondered the weight of mortality as I took the stairs down
from my fourth floor walk-up.

Near sundown, I had completed my appointed rounds and
was making my way up Avenida San Pablo toward my
apartment. All over the crowded streets of El Centro
Histórico there are vendors, called "coyotes" because they
are not legally licensed, hawking a vast array of wares,
everything from roasted ears of corn to dice to rabbit-ear
television antennas, and then some. If it exists, it is some-

where on the streets of El Centro. A great number of these coyotes sell CDs, pirated of course, for ten pesos each, or about $1 U.S., and passing through the small park at the Pino Suarez metro stop, I noticed a fellow I had not seen before. (Coyotes pretty much stay on the move.) He had a table of CDs that caught my attention, because his entire stock was American blues, an excellent cross-section of the genre, with a few fairly obscure artists. I wondered, for instance, how many copies of Snooky Pryor this guy could sell in a week—hell, in a year.

As I browsed, a picture of George Harrison caught my eye. I picked up the CD and read the title: *Rock Legends, George Harrison with Eric Clapton and His Band, Fourth Night Live, Rock Legends Japan Tour '91.* I asked the guy how much he wanted for it, and he told me eighty pesos.

"Wow," I mumbled.

"But, señor," he said, "it is a two-CD set."

"Yeah," I said. "You're right."

As I reached into my pocket to see how much cash I had with me, I said, "George died today. Did you know that?"

"Sí, señor," the coyote said, "I have heard the news. I am sad in my heart."

"Sí, señor," I said, "So am I."

And I handed him a 100-peso bill.